more night
Whispers

For information on scheduling Jennie Afman Dimkoff to speak to your organization, go to her website at:

www.storylineministries.com
or contact Speak Up Speaker Services
toll free: (888) 870-7719

more night Whispers

bedtime
Bible stories
for women

Jennie Afman Dimkoff

Revell
Grand Rapids, Michigan

Published by Fleming H. Revell
a division of Baker Book House Company
P.O. Box 6287, Grand Rapids, MI 49516-6287
www.bakerbooks.com

Printed in the United States of America

Library of Congress Cataloging-in-Publication Data
Dimkoff, Jennie Afman.
    More night whispers : bedtime Bible stories for women / Jennie Afman Dimkoff.
        p.   cm.
    Includes bibliographical references.
    ISBN 0-8007-1835-6 (hardcover)
    1. Bible stories, English. 2. Women—Prayer-books and devotions—English.
  I. Title.
  BS550.3.D55 2004
  242′.643—dc22   2004001246

This book is lovingly dedicated
to my sister and precious friend
Carol Kent

Remember being bed pals as kids
and whispering into the night?
Remember our earnest prayer as children
that others would actually see
the love of Jesus on our faces?
We were young girls when God captured our hearts
and we surrendered our lives to him.
Since that time we've laughed and cried together,
and as the years went by we sang duets as teenagers
and teamed in ministry as adults.
Summer after summer we've walked on beaches together
and shared our deepest thoughts.
You have loved, mentored, and encouraged me
for my entire lifetime,
and today you are a remarkable example
of how to reflect Christ
and reach out to others with his love,
even through heartache.
You are an incredible woman, and I love you.

Contents

Acknowledgments

Writing this book was a tremendous learning experience for me as I researched and wrote each chapter. Although I cannot claim to be a Bible scholar, I dearly love God's Word and deeply desire to share it with others. In retelling the ancient stories for a twenty-first-century readership, I stayed as close as possible to the original text, while still giving myself the author's luxury of creating a setting or adding what I felt was appropriate dialogue. The finished project is due to the assistance and faithful support of many, and I am greatly indebted to the following people.

The Revell publishing team: Thank you for believing in this project and taking a risk on the first *Night Whispers* book. Jennifer Leep, Kristin Kornoelje, Twila Bennett, Ruth Waybrant, Cheryl VanAndel, Karen Steele, and Marilyn Gordon—what an amazing team you are! Your warmth and enthusiasm have been such an encouragement to me.

Dr. Robert W. Nienhuis, executive vice president of Cornerstone University: Your careful and qualified review of my manuscript for biblical accuracy was a significant time commitment on your part, for which I am deeply thankful. Thank you for your words of affirmation and, at the same time, for challenging the storyteller in me to stay true to God's Word.

Those who allowed me to share their stories: In addition to retelling ancient Bible stories, it was my desire to offer a contemporary story in each chapter to help the reader better identify with the biblical story. Some stories were from my own personal experience, but many dear friends and family members allowed me to tell their stories as well. In places the names have been changed to guard their privacy, but the stories themselves are told with their blessing. Thank you all for your special contributions to this manuscript.

My ministry assistants: Linda Goorhouse, your assistance in my office during the writing of this manuscript was priceless. Thank you for Xeroxing hundreds of pages of research for me to study while I was "on the road," for helping to keep me on schedule, and for being such a blessing to work with.

Jan Zimmerman, as my prayer partner and ministry traveling companion, you are the dearest friend, driver, road manager, and most enthusiastic book table organizer I could possibly have been blessed with! I am so grateful to you and to your husband, Ed, for your faithful friendship and loyalty to this ministry.

My family and praying friends: Graydon Dimkoff, you are my husband, best friend, and encourager. Thanks for helping me to find creative getaway places to study and write and for being willing to do without me when I was away or in the throes of writing. Amber Joy, your phone calls, manuscript review, and stories were a constant encouragement to me. Josh, your commitment to Christ thrills me, and your enthusiasm for my writing is a joy to my heart. I love you, dear family.

To my parents and praying friends, I offer grateful thanks. Please continue to pray that God will use this book to draw many unto himself.

Introduction

My niece, an irresistible little redhead named Lucy, spent the day before her fourth birthday with me. We filled the morning with craft projects produced at my kitchen table. We colored, glued, and adorned our masterpieces with silly stickers and glitter, but her favorite activity by far was stringing hard candy necklaces and tying them around our necks.

After lunch we donned our aprons (I keep a small one in my kitchen drawer expressly for her visits), pulled up a stool to position her at the right height for the kitchen counter, and frosted her birthday cupcakes, still wearing our lovely necklaces, of course. When the job was completed, I scraped the last remnant of frosting from the bowl and handed Lucy the rubber spatula.

"Hey, little Miss Lucy, do you want a lick?"

Lucy nodded, reached eagerly for the treat, and immediately dragged her tongue over the daub of chocolate. Then looking up at me with a big grin and chocolate between her teeth, she said, "Aunt Jennie, you're my kind of woman!"

The moment was priceless. And it reminded me of someone else. You.

Thanks for picking up this book. You may not be wearing a candy necklace or licking chocolate from a spatula at this moment, but if you love to curl up at the end of the day with a good book and find yourself caught up in a great story, you're my kind of woman. And if you've ever picked up a Bible and wondered how those ancient stories could possibly be relevant to your life today, believe me, I've been there too.

Are you ready? We're about to step within the pages of ten intriguing stories retold from the Bible, the most life-changing book of all time. Walk through the stories with the ancient characters who lived them, and gain a deeper understanding of the lessons they learned and how those principles can apply to your own life today. You may relate to the contemporary story at the end of each chapter and find hope and direction in the "Whispered Prayer" and "Get Up and Go Ideas for Tomorrow" sections. As you experience each story and ponder its relevance, don't forget to listen for God's whisper. I'm praying that you'll allow him to touch your heart.

Happy reading, sweet dreams, and don't forget to turn out the light!

Jennie Afman Dimkoff

I hear this most gentle whisper from One I never guessed would speak to me.

Psalm 81:5 MESSAGE

ONE

The Awakening

A Story about Innocence, Loss, and Lessons Learned

Christy awoke slowly, savoring the knowledge that she was finally *here*. Her roommate had already left their dorm room, but in the stillness, Christy's thoughts were anything but quiet. She was at the University of Michigan, and classes would begin today. Her life would finally begin!

Raised and home-schooled by loving but protective parents, Christy was finally on her own. While thoughts of the farm and rural community where she had been raised were comforting, the adventure and freedom that awaited her were almost intoxicating.

As she swung her legs off the bed to get up, she caught a glimpse of her Bible on her desk. She'd been too tired after moving in to spend time with God the first night she was here. Yesterday she'd been busy scrambling around buying her books and figuring out where her classes would be, and then last night she had been invited to attend two sorority parties for Rush Week. She didn't know if she would pledge or not, but it had been exciting to be included. After sleeping in this morning, she didn't have a moment to open her Bible now. It would have to wait.

Leaving the dorm, Christy swung her backpack behind her, threaded her arms through the straps, and headed for her first class.

"Hey! Wait up!"

Turning toward the beckoning call, Christy stopped in her tracks. Unbidden, the thought struck her. *Oh, my goodness. He is gorgeous!*

"You heading to the music building?" the male voice asked.

Christy nodded dumbly, and, to her annoyance, an uncontrollable blush burned its way from her neck to cover her face.

"Great! I'll just tag along and keep you company. My name's Ramone Santana. Of course, my close friends call me Romeo," he added with an exaggerated wink. "You're Christy, right?"

At her incredulous look he grinned, an irresistible dimple denting one cheek. "I pestered your roommate at the party last night until she told me your name. Hey, you're blushing!" He lowered his voice and leaned so close that she could feel the warmth of his breath on her cheek. "Your innocence is very attractive to me, Christy. I'd like to see you this weekend."

For a moment Christy felt uneasy, but she quickly brushed the feeling aside. He was so much fun! She didn't pause to wonder if Ramone had her best interests at heart.

Tossing her hair back, she regarded him for a moment and then smiled. "Maybe," she said with a twinkle in her eye. It was fun to flirt. "We'll see, won't we?"

TEMPTATION COMES PACKAGED in many different forms, and Christy's story about innocence abroad for the first time is not unlike the story of another young woman in history. Actually, she's also the first woman in history. Her name was Eve. While some paint her as a temptress, she had an undeniable innocence and naivety about her that were unparalleled in any other woman born after her. She was also vulnerable and fell prey to a persuasive tempter. The choice she made and others that followed would change the course of humankind.

Step into the garden with me to observe the "awakening" of Eve, the mother of us all.

Eve's Story

So still. Adam watched the scene before him with intense interest. The very sight of the woman filled him with an un-speakable joy. She was beautiful—perfectly proportioned but utterly still. He held his own breath while the Creator gently cradled her head between the hands that had formed her and breathed into her the breath of life.

Her body jolted for a moment, and her chest expanded as the rush of life-giving air filled her lungs. Her lips parted in a gasp, and although she hadn't yet opened her eyes, the lids twitched slightly. As her breathing evened, her lips took on a rosy hue—the same delightful phenomenon soon stained her cheeks. A finger moved against the bed of grass upon which she was lying, and then others. Her eyes fluttered open, and a look of wonder soon turned to joy as a smile lit her countenance.

Adam could understand exactly what she was experiencing, because his own "birth" had occurred in much the same way. She was seeing the Creator for the first time and was washed in the glory of his presence. There would never be a moment like it again.

Awe and gratitude overwhelmed him. Unconsciously Adam rubbed his hand over the place on his side where the Creator had taken one of his ribs to use in forming this exquisite creature who was so like him but yet so different. Words sprang involuntarily to his lips.

"She's beautiful!"

At the sound of his voice, the woman turned and looked at him for the first time.

MANY DAYS LATER, rays of morning sun touched her sleeping form curled beneath the fig tree. Adam had already awakened and left their mattress of soft grass to oversee the animals in the garden. He enjoyed the work Creator God had given him and looked forward to it each new day. He loved the animals and took joy in recognizing the uniqueness of each one God had made.

But this morning when he woke, like every morning since the woman had been created, he paused to stare at her with awe that left him swallowing hard with a grateful emotion he hardly understood. He took such joy in exploring the garden with her, in introducing her to each of the animals, and in watching her delight when an elephant sprayed water from its trunk or when the cougar rubbed against her leg, begging for affection. Such a gift God had given him in her. Bone of his bone, flesh of his flesh, they were one.

THE WOMAN STIRRED and inhaled deeply. Rolling over, she became aware of sunlight resting on her closed eyelids. For a moment, it reminded her of the first time she had opened her eyes in this garden. Her very first conscious thought had been an awareness of the warmth and brightness of the presence of Creator God. The corners of her lips lifted at the memory, and she opened her eyes with a smile. Above her, broad leaves harbored ripe figs, and at the thought, she felt her stomach growl. This was a new day, and she and Adam would walk with the Creator just after the sun set, in the cool of the early evening. It was the highlight of every day.

Reaching her arms above her head, she stiffened her body in a wake-up stretch that reached all the way to her toes. What a perfect place this was! If she listened carefully, she could hear so many different things. There was the sound of the brook as water rushed over the stones until it reached the clear pond at the bottom of the hill. She had taken Adam's hand and followed the brook's gurgling path the very first day she had been here. She had been so delighted to see blue, gold, and coral-colored fish swimming in the pond, and had laughed out loud with surprise when one jumped right up out of the water and landed back with a splash. Listening again, she could hear the call of the monkeys and the rustling of leaves as they chased one another in the trees. Her favorite sound, however, was the chorus of birds that welcomed her each morning. Would she ever learn all their names or be able to identify each call like Adam could?

Thinking of her beloved, she stood and, shading her eyes from the eastern sun, sought Adam. He was probably near the caves to the south of the garden, where the lions had made their den. Last night he had told her that the female would soon bear a cub. She knew Adam would want to be near to praise and encourage the mother as she gave birth and to welcome and name the little one. Since the Creator had commanded the fish and birds to fill the sea and sky and the animals to fill the earth, the miracle of birth filled each day with drama and wonder. Adam's job as caretaker was no small undertaking, and the woman, as his helper, especially loved the newborn animals.

Eager to discover what this new day held in store, the woman headed for the pond. Later she combed her fingers though her wet hair and, tucking an orchid behind one ear, set off through the lush foliage to find her mate.

STEPPING INTO THE CLEARING, the woman stopped for a moment to look around with fresh wonder at the colors and feather-like ferns surrounding the area. At the center of the clearing was a beautiful tree, majestic in proportion, lush with leaves of a unique pattern with which she was unfamiliar, and heavy-laden with fruit. Had she ever seen this part of the garden before?

Ah, yes, she thought. *This is the Tree of the Knowledge of Good and Evil. Adam and I have walked with God here in the evening. It looks quite different in the sunlight; truly spectacular.*

MESMERIZED BY THE SIGHT before her, the woman was unaware that she was being observed by someone else. Satan, the enemy of the Creator, had made his way into the garden, disguising himself by assuming the form of the serpent, one of the most interesting of God's creations. Satan knew that the naive woman had been fascinated by the creature in days past, with its fluid gracefulness and its iridescent colors that changed in the sunlight.

"Hello, Beautiful," he whispered.

STARTLED, THE WOMAN turned toward a voice beckoning to her from the tree. "Adam? Where are you? I was on my way to find you."

"Over here."

The voice seemed to be drawing her closer to the tree. As the woman approached, she noticed that a serpent had wrapped his body around the base of the tree. The creature raised up in one fluid movement until he was balanced upright, watching her at her eye level.

What a magnificent creature this is, the woman thought, fascinated by its changing colors and the gentle rocking motion it was making in midair.

"This is a beautiful place, isn't it? And this tree . . . it's like none other in the garden." The creature smiled as he spoke to her.

"You spoke!"

"Indeed I did," the serpent replied.

The woman, at first surprised, was then delighted by this unusual phenomenon.

"What a wise creature you are! I wonder if Adam knows that you can speak as we do?"

"Is that where you're headed? To find Adam?" the serpent asked conversationally.

When she nodded, the creature continued. "Have you eaten yet this morning?" he asked.

The woman shook her head and immediately felt a hunger pang move through her stomach. "I should have picked figs and eaten them on the way," she answered and then shrugged. "The garden has fruit in abundance. I'll just find something else."

"Have you considered the fruit of this magnificent tree?" the serpent asked.

"Oh no! I couldn't!" The woman took a step back.

"Why not?" the creature asked, moving his body seductively up the trunk of the tree and out on a limb near the woman. "Ah, you should smell it! The aroma makes my mouth water."

"The fruit of that tree is forbidden," the woman stated firmly, shaking her head back and forth. "God gave us permission to eat of every tree in the garden except this one. We must not even touch it or we will die!"

"And why do you think he said that?" the serpent asked, laughing gently. It was an oddly comforting laugh, and it soothed the woman's nervousness. She had never felt nervous before.

"You will not surely die. You see, my dear, God knows that when you taste this fruit your eyes will be opened, and you will be like God, knowing good and evil. My own eyes have certainly been opened." He laughed softly again. "You should taste and see for yourself how delicious and desirable this fruit really is."

The woman looked from the serpent to a lush piece of fruit hanging just above her. Its skin was shiny and sparkled in the sunlight. She felt her stomach growl once more, and her mouth watered. But it was far more than a physical hunger she felt. She was very curious about this *knowledge* the serpent talked about.

With a trembling hand, she reached up and plucked the fruit. She turned and saw the serpent watching her, his eyes gleaming.

"See? You touched the tree and nothing happened! Didn't I tell you that God was just keeping the best for himself? Now, go on. Take a bite of the best fruit you've ever tasted!"

The woman wavered, but temptation overwhelmed her. Her strong white teeth pierced the crisp skin of the fruit as she took her first bite. Sweet juice ran down her chin. "Mmm," she murmured, licking her lips and smiling at the serpent before taking another bite.

"Hey, wait a minute!" the serpent said. "Aren't you forgetting someone?"

The woman paused, holding the treat in midair.

"Weren't you on your way to find Adam? Don't you want to share the best with him?"

The woman nodded and grinned, casually reached up, and plucked another piece of fruit.

ADAM GRINNED with pleasure when he saw the woman coming to meet him. Her cheeks were flushed with excitement.

"Adam, I've brought you a surprise! Wait until you see!"

Her expression was different than he'd ever seen before. A little bolder. Fun. She was often fun, but today she was *sassy*. "Just wait until you taste!" she exclaimed, her eyes sparkling as she held out a piece of fruit.

A hint of alarm ran through him, but her mood was contagious and he reached out for the treat. "Where did you get this?"

"Well . . . I was on my way to find you and ended up in the center of the garden. The serpent was there, and Adam, he talked to me! He explained that this fruit was delicious and absolutely safe to eat. That I certainly wouldn't die, in fact, I'd become as—"

"No!" Adam shouted. "You took this fruit from the Tree of Knowledge? You know it's forbidden!"

THE WOMAN WAS SHOCKED. Adam had never spoken to her like that before. What was this? Why did he use that tone of voice? Reaching out to him and laughing nervously, she tried to calm him.

"Adam, look at me. I'm fine, just like the serpent said I would be. I didn't die. Not only that, he said I would become like God himself and know good and evil. Don't you want that too? It was absolutely delicious, and I wanted to share this wonderful secret with you too. You must be starving after leaving so early this morning. Here, my love. Refresh yourself."

THE FRUIT DID SMELL GOOD. He couldn't place the scent, but it made his mouth water. Adam knew without doubt that he was acting in disobedience to God, but was it really that big a deal?

He shrugged his nagging conscience aside and took a bite. Delicious! Laughing, he and the woman finished the treat and came together in an embrace.

BUT SOMETHING WAS very wrong. Their mood instantly changed. Pulling apart, they stared at one another for a moment, and then, looking down at their own bodies, they were overwhelmed with an ugly feeling of shame that was so alien it left them terrified. The woman dropped to the ground, pulling her hair around her in a pitiful attempt to cover her nakedness. Adam turned his back to her, trying to hide himself too. He could hear her sobbing.

What has happened to us? he thought frantically. *Where is the joyful, carefree innocence we knew? This is the "knowledge" we desired? What fools we have been!*

Running for the forest, Adam could think only of covering himself. The fig tree under which they had spent so many precious nights together had large broad leaves, and he gathered a pile together with long strands of ivy. Stripping the leaves from the ivy, he clumsily threaded the fig leaves together to make an apron of sorts to cover his nakedness. Then he made another and went back to find his wife. His heart broke when he found her, still crouched on the ground but filthy from digging at the earth around her to cover herself with bits of grass and dirt. Her grimy face was streaked with tears.

THEY WAITED IN TERRIFIED SILENCE for the day to end. In the cool of the evening they heard the sound of the Lord God as he

22

walked in the garden. Rather than running to meet him, they hid themselves instead.

"Adam! Where are you?" God called.

The voice was right beside them. Suddenly Adam understood that the God who had created him knew exactly where he was but was patiently waiting for him to come forward. Crawling awkwardly from under the leafy foliage and keeping his eyes on the ground, he answered the Creator. The woman cowered behind him.

"I'm here, Lord. I heard your voice, but I was frightened because of my nakedness, so I hid myself."

"How did you know you were naked?" the Creator asked. "Have you eaten from the tree I commanded you not to eat from?"

Adam trembled before the Lord God and thought frantically for an excuse. "Ah . . . ah, the woman you put here with me—she gave me some fruit from the tree, and I ate it."

CREATOR GOD LOOKED at the woman. "What is this you have done?"

She felt faint and tried to wet her lips with a dry tongue. "The serpent deceived me. I believed his lies, and I ate."

There was silence for a moment. A terrifying silence. Turning to the serpent waiting smugly off to the side, God cursed him to crawl on his belly and eat dirt forever. "There will be hatred between you and the woman, and between your offspring and hers; he will crush your head, and you will strike his heel!"

Turning to the woman he said, "I will greatly increase your pains in childbirth. . . . You will desire your husband, but he will rule over you."

Pain? the woman thought frantically. *What is this pain the Creator is talking about? And hatred between me and the serpent?*

She already felt bitter animosity toward the serpent, which was now writhing on the ground, but what did God mean about her offspring crushing the serpent's head? This was all so frightening and confusing.

And then, facing Adam, God said, "I commanded you not to eat from the Tree of Knowledge of Good and Evil. You understood that, Adam, but because you listened to your wife and chose to eat of it anyway, cursed is the ground because of you; through painful toil you will eat of it all of the days of your life. It will produce thorns and thistles for you, and you will eat the plants of the field. By the sweat of your brow you will eat your food until you return to the ground, since from it you were taken, for dust you are and to dust you will return."

THE WOMAN CLUNG to Adam before the presence of the Lord. As he held her, a dreadful calm settled on Adam's soul—the reality of their sin was sinking in. Cupping her tear-stained face, he lovingly performed his first act of authority over the woman God had given to him. "Your name shall be Eve," he said, a bittersweet smile touching his face for a moment, "because you will become the mother of all humankind."

THAT NIGHT WOULD be their last in the garden, and it was not a peaceful one. For the first time peace was shattered by the sound of animals screaming. For the first time blood was spilled in paradise. The Lord God sacrificed animals precious to him and to them and made leather garments in place of the inadequate aprons to cover Adam and Eve's nakedness, their shame. It had grieved them all.

Then the Lord God said, "The man now knows good and evil. In his sinful state he must not be allowed to also reach out his hand and eat from the Tree of Life, for then he would live forever.

Therefore, man will be banished from this place, and will have to work the ground from which he was taken to survive."

Their cries and pleas were futile. Once Adam and Eve were driven from the garden, God placed a powerful angelic warrior with a sword that flashed back and forth at the East Gate to guard the way to the Tree of Life.

Their sin had cost so much. Innocence lost. Paradise lost. Intimacy with God lost. But God, in his great love for humankind, had a plan. In the end, there would be salvation.

Digging Deeper

Did you know that the book of Genesis literally sets the stage for everything we read about later in the Bible? It is the book of beginnings. In the early chapters we read of the beginning of the universe, the earth, people, the family unit, evil and sin, salvation and redemption. I chose to begin this book with the story of the creation of Eve, the first woman, and the choice she made that would affect the life of every woman after her.

Take a look at the key elements of the story with me.

The setting? The Garden of Eden. It was paradise physically, spiritually, and emotionally, but where was it located? The exact location isn't known, but in several places the Bible gives pieces of geographical information that would point to a site in the Middle East. According to scholars, it may have been located in Mesopotamia, which is modern-day Iraq.[1]

It was a place of lush foliage and no weeds. It was a place where it never rained (but the Bible says a mist would rise up from the ground and water the garden). It was a place of unimaginable beauty and peace but also of responsibility, joy, fellowship with God, and free will. Can you imagine a place with no heartache, fear, anger, conflict, need, or regrets? That's what it was like—until sin crept in.

Adam and Eve were perfect companions. You've heard the expression "they're made for each other"? Well, that's exactly the case here—God made Eve for Adam to be his companion, his helper, his friend, his wife, his lover. We don't know how long Adam had been alive before God created Eve, but it had been long enough to name all the animals and to understand his job as resident "caretaker" of the garden. God knew that Adam needed someone and that he shouldn't be alone.

It is easy to imagine Adam and Eve running hand in hand as he introduced her to the garden, to each of the animals, and to each type of vegetation and fruit. I picture their fingers stained with berries or with the juice of sweet, tree-ripened peaches dripping off their chins and onto their bellies. Heading for a clear pool of water with large lily pads floating on the surface, they would dive and resurface, automatically reaching out for each other. And in the evenings, they would literally walk with God. Paradise.

The sin? Disobedience to God. I wonder how long it took Satan to wear down Eve's resistance. A day, a week, a year? Regardless of how long she debated the decision, she made the choice to disobey God, ate the fruit, and introduced her husband to the forbidden treat. "The first couple gained a terrible new knowledge by breaking the rules. After eating the fruit, Adam and Eve, who had previously known only good, now came to know evil."[2] With their sin came the terrible loss of innocence, leaving them shocked, bereft, and ashamed. Reading their story brought to my mind the tragedy of a little boy's loss of innocence and the emotional and physical toll a father's sin took on a young life.

Diana and Kyle had two young children. Diana was a physician and Kyle a respected businessman—they were the picture of success. But their friends at church had no idea that Kyle struggled with both cocaine and pornography addictions. He refused counseling, and when the children grew older and Kyle's binges became more frequent, Diana filed for divorce, convinced she was taking a firm step that would protect their children.

Several days later, Diana's eleven-year-old son approached her, looking ill.

"Mom, is this Dad's writing?" he asked in a quiet voice.

"Honey, are you all right?" Alarmed, Diana looked down and saw that her son was holding a stack of graphically pornographic photographs printed off the Internet. The disgusting notes added to the pages were indeed in her husband's handwriting.

"Oh, honey." Dismayed, she struggled to find the right words to say. "That rotten stuff belongs in the trash." Before she could even dispose of the photos, her shocked child was vomiting. There was nothing physically wrong with him, no fever, no symptoms of any illness. But he was soul-sick to the point of throwing up.

I imagine that's how Adam and Eve felt. Sick and shamed to the depths of their souls. I wonder—could they hear the serpent laughing at them as they hid in the bushes?

The sentence? Expulsion from Paradise. But why did they have to leave the garden? Because God could not allow sinful man access to the Tree of Life, which would have enabled them to live forever in a fallen condition.

The sentence was a curse. God punished the serpent first and humbled him to the ground. As for Eve, she would desire her husband, but she would bear their children in pain and come under her husband's authority. And weeds and endless work were the punishment for Adam. Every generation of men and women to follow would experience the same.

Don't think for a moment that God enjoyed the cursing. He fully realized that the ultimate price for their sin would one day be paid with the life of his own Son, Jesus.

The sacrifice? God sacrificed the life of one or more of the animals that he and Adam loved and cared for to make leather garments to cover their nakedness and shame. Think how heartbreaking that must have been for them both! Then the Scripture says that God "clothed them" (Gen. 3:21). Max Lucado, in his book *A Love Worth Giving*, describes what that moment might have been like, and its significance to each of us.

Adam and Eve are on their way out of the garden. They've been told to leave, but now God tells them to stop. "Those fig leaves," he says, shaking his head, "will never do." And he produces some clothing. But he doesn't throw the garments at their feet and tell them to get dressed. He dresses them himself. Hold still, Adam, let's see how this fits. . . . God covers them. He protects them.

Love always protects.

Hasn't he done the same for us? We eat our share of forbidden fruit. We say what we shouldn't say. Go where we shouldn't go. Pluck fruit from trees we shouldn't touch.

And when we do, the door opens and shame tumbles in. And we hide. We sew fig leaves. Flimsy excuses. See-through justifications. We cover ourselves in good works and good deeds, but one gust of the wind of truth, and we are naked again—stark naked in our own failure.

So what does God do? Exactly what he did for our parents in the garden. He sheds innocent blood. He offers the life of his Son. And from the scene of the sacrifice the Father takes a robe—not the skin of an animal—but the robe of righteousness. And does he throw it in our direction and tell us to shape up? No, he dresses us himself. He dresses us with himself.[3]

It is interesting to note that in the Old Testament one of the meanings of the expression "to atone" is "to cover."[4] By covering Adam and Eve before expelling them from the garden, God showed his *grace* before his *judgment*. What a wonderful relief!

The silver lining? Hope for a Savior. How little did Eve realize when God's judgment was poured out on her that she was given an awesome promise as well. When God said that one day the serpent would be crushed by the seed of the woman, he was promising a redeemer, a savior.

Throughout her lifetime Eve endured physical hardship, pain in childbirth, the guilt of knowing that her sin would be passed on to her children, and the heartbreaking grief of having one of her sons murder his own brother. But Eve never lost hope, and she did not feel abandoned by God. When she delivered her first son in Genesis 4:1, she rejoiced in her precious gift from the Lord. She without doubt gave birth to many children in her lifetime, and at the end of the record of her story she gives birth to Seth, her last son named in Scripture. (Since Adam was 130 years old at the time, I imagine she was somewhere around that age as well.) She once again recognized that the child was a special gift from God. He would not be the savior she hoped for, but from his lineage Jesus the Savior would one day come. A Savior for us all.

How can this story apply to your life?

The unfinished scenario of Christy at the beginning of this chapter left her flirting with obvious temptation. Her choice could lead her down one path or another. Her story is unfinished—just like ours. Every day we're faced with temptations. Like Eve, we've all made wrong choices in the past and have had to face the consequences or accept the responsibility for our actions.

Learn from Eve by remembering that God loves you and has a plan for your life (even when you mess up). Eve confessed her sin to God (Gen. 3:13), and then went on with life, continuing to turn to him for help (Gen. 4:1).

God created human beings, not puppets, and we are free to choose how to live our lives. Someone once wrote, "When we follow through on our impulses, the satisfaction we find is hollow and vanishes quickly."[5] I believe this is often true. Think back to some of the impulsive acts you have committed in the past that left you with emptiness rather than satisfaction. What did you lose from your mistake? What did you learn?

Recognize that God is longing for a relationship with you. Even when we make a mess of things and later are so ashamed that we'd like to hide, he's calling our names. *"Jennie, where are you?"* Oh, he knows where we are, all right. The God who created us is just waiting for us to seek his face, confess our sin, and accept his forgiveness and the robe of righteousness that is ours because of the sacrifice of his Son Jesus on the cross. "We hide. He seeks. We bring sin. He brings a sacrifice. We try fig leaves. He brings the robe of righteousness. . . . God has clothed us. He protects us with a cloak of love."[6]

I GREW UP in a family of six children. Five of us were girls, and there was never much peace and quiet in our home. Most people think that when you grow up in a parsonage like I did, it's paradise, right? A place where peace is personified and harmony reigns. Actually, that's not how I would describe our home. We squabbled over time on the telephone, whose turn it was to do the dishes, who saw that boy first, and who really owned that outfit. Our dad laid down the law, and Mama buttered it up with love.

When I was in the second grade, I attended a small country school. I was a good student for the most part, but one day the teacher announced that at the end of the hour we would be having a spelling test. I panicked. I didn't know the words! I'd get them all wrong! What could I do? I anguished over the problem until I listened to a little voice in my head that offered a solution to my dilemma.

I could copy the words down on a piece of paper and hide it in my hand. Then, when it came time for the test, I could peek at the paper, copy the words down, and get them all right!

That's just what I did. The teacher called out the words, and I nervously peeked at the paper, copied the words, and got a perfect paper. The only problem was that the girl beside me saw and, waving her arm in the air, told the teacher. (The girl's name was Cookie—I will never forget it!)

In my humiliation I cried and I lied, saying vehemently that I hadn't done it. I wadded that piece of paper into a tiny knot, dropped it to the floor, and put my foot on it so nobody would see it.

I went home on the bus that day in misery and then went upstairs to be miserable alone. In the meantime, my big sister Carol, who also attended class at the little schoolhouse, told Mother everything that had happened at school that day.

Our parents had never been ones to "spare the rod and spoil the child," but in this instance, Mother waited . . . until the next morning. When I woke up, it was still early, and I thought everyone else was asleep. I had an awful bellyache. I just knew I wasn't well enough to go to school.

I went downstairs in the silent house, and to my surprise Mama was waiting for me in the kitchen. "Jennie," she asked quietly, "is there something you ought to tell me?"

"No, Mama," I mumbled nervously, shaking my head slightly.

"Jennie, are you sure there's not something you want to tell me?" she asked again.

"No, Mama," I whispered, studying the floor.

"Come here, Jennie."

Mother had a built-in lie detector. She had a method for extracting the truth, and it was infallible. We called it the "Thumb Test." We had to stand before her, look up into her quiet, blue eyes, and hold out a thumb. Taking the thumb in her hand, she would hold it—not twist it or pinch it or hurt it in any way, just hold it. Then as she asked her question (regarding whatever truth she happened to be seeking), she would s-l-o-w-l-y begin to rub our thumb with her thumb. There was no way you could look into Mother's eyes and feel her rubbing your thumb and tell a lie. We knew it was magic.

I burst into tears that morning and confessed my sins. How first I had cheated and then I had lied. What did Mother do then? She didn't say a word. Sitting down in the kitchen rocker, she took me in her arms, gently put her face against mine, and, as we rocked, she cried.

Do you have any idea what it did to my young, second grade heart to see and hear my mother weeping over my sin? It broke it in two. We cried for a while, then we wiped our eyes, blew our noses, and prayed. I told God how sorry I was for being a cheat and a liar and for shaming him. I asked him to help me not do anything like that again.

I felt so much better. But that wasn't the end of the lesson.

"Now you'll have to go to school and tell the teacher," Mother stated quietly.

"Oh no, Mama. I just can't. Couldn't you tell her for me?" I pleaded.

"No, you'll have to do it yourself," she insisted.

Somehow that morning my mother made arrangements for the care of the other children, arranged to use the family car, and drove me to the schoolhouse before anyone else arrived. My heart was thudding as I waited for the teacher.

When her car pulled in, I jumped out of ours and ran across the gravel parking lot, throwing my arms around my beloved teacher's knees. Then as I looked up I said, "Oh, Teacher, yesterday I cheated and I lied, but today I asked God to forgive me. Will you forgive me too?"

That dear, tenderhearted woman stooped down, put her arms around me . . . and cried too! I was forgiven! Forgiven! It was wonderful. A two-ton weight of guilt lifted off second grade shoulders that day, and I learned a lesson that would last me a lifetime. It was twofold: First, I learned the importance of a contrite heart as described in Psalms—a sorry heart for my sin. Second, I learned about the relief and the incredible joy that comes with forgiveness.

And why did I learn this lesson? Because I had a mother who wisely and lovingly dealt with my wrongdoing. Even though it made her sad, she took a firm but loving action that would teach me a lesson for a lifetime. She cared more about my development than my embarrassment or her disappointment. Kind of reminds me of our Creator God.

A Whispered Prayer

Dear Heavenly Father, you know better than anyone that I am far from perfect. Thank you for loving me anyway! I confess that I am a sinner. Please help me learn from my mistakes rather than repeat them. Help me to realize that the consequences that may seem painful or embarrassing at the moment may be just the lesson that will be a turning point in my life. Help me to accept responsibility for my actions and to make wise choices in the future. In the precious name of Jesus, Amen.

Get Up and Go Ideas for Tomorrow

1. I will read Eve's story from the Bible in Genesis 2:19–4:25. (You can read this passage in your own Bible or refer to the scriptural text at the end of this chapter.)

2. As I encounter temptation tomorrow, whether it's flirting with someone I shouldn't, using a substance that's harmful to me, or saying or doing something I know is wrong (to name just a few possibilities), I won't act on impulse! I will pause and ask God to help me make choices that are right for me and pleasing to him.

A Thought to Ponder as I Fall Asleep

Do I flirt with temptations or do I turn away from them?

The Scripture Reading: Genesis 2:7–3:24

The Lord God formed the man from the dust of the ground and breathed into his nostrils the breath of life, and the man became a living being.

Now the Lord God had planted a garden in the east, in Eden; and there he put the man he had formed. And the Lord God made all kinds of trees grow out of the ground—trees that were pleasing to the eye and good for food. In the middle of the garden were the tree of life and the tree of the knowledge of good and evil.

A river watering the garden flowed from Eden; from there it was separated into four headwaters. The name of the first is the Pishon; it winds through the entire land of Havilah, where there is gold. (The gold of that land is good; aromatic resin and onyx are also there.) The name of the second river is the Gihon; it winds through the entire land of Cush. The name of the third river is the Tigris; it runs along the east side of Asshur. And the fourth river is the Euphrates.

The Lord God took the man and put him in the Garden of Eden to work it and take care of it. And the Lord God commanded the man, "You are free to eat from any tree in the garden; but you must not eat from the tree of the knowledge of good and evil, for when you eat of it you will surely die."

The Lord God said, "It is not good for the man to be alone. I will make a helper suitable for him."

Now the Lord God had formed out of the ground all the beasts of the field and all the birds of the air. He brought them to the man to see what he would name them; and whatever the man called each living creature, that was its name. So the man gave names to all the livestock, the birds of the air and all the beasts of the field.

But for Adam no suitable helper was found. So the Lord God caused the man to fall into a deep sleep; and while he was sleeping, he took one of the man's ribs and closed up the place with flesh. Then the Lord God made a woman from the rib he had taken out of the man, and he brought her to the man.

The man said,

"This is now bone of my bones
    and flesh of my flesh;
she shall be called 'woman,'
    for she was taken out of man."

For this reason a man will leave his father and mother and be united to his wife, and they will become one flesh.

The man and his wife were both naked, and they felt no shame.

Now the serpent was more crafty than any of the wild animals the Lord God had made. He said to the woman, "Did God really say, 'You must not eat from any tree in the garden'?"

The woman said to the serpent, "We may eat fruit from the trees in the garden, but God did say, 'You must not eat fruit from the tree that is in the middle of the garden, and you must not touch it, or you will die.'"

"You will not surely die," the serpent said to the woman. "For God knows that when you eat of it your eyes will be opened, and you will be like God, knowing good and evil."

When the woman saw that the fruit of the tree was good for food and pleasing to the eye, and also desirable for gaining wisdom, she took some and ate it. She also gave some to her husband, who was with her, and he ate it. Then the eyes of both of them were opened, and they realized they were naked; so they sewed fig leaves together and made coverings for themselves.

Then the man and his wife heard the sound of the Lord God as he was walking in the garden in the cool of the day, and they hid from the Lord God among the trees of the garden. But the Lord God called to the man, "Where are you?"

He answered, "I heard you in the garden, and I was afraid because I was naked; so I hid."

And he said, "Who told you that you were naked? Have you eaten from the tree that I commanded you not to eat from?"

The man said, "The woman you put here with me—she gave me some fruit from the tree, and I ate it."

Then the Lord God said to the woman, "What is this you have done?"

The woman said, "The serpent deceived me, and I ate."

So the Lord God said to the serpent, "Because you have done this,

"Cursed are you above all the livestock
and all the wild animals!
You will crawl on your belly
and you will eat dust
all the days of your life.
And I will put enmity
between you and the woman,
and between your offspring and
hers;
he will crush your head,
and you will strike his heel."

To the woman he said,

"I will greatly increase your pains in
childbearing;
with pain you will give birth to
children.
Your desire will be for your husband,
and he will rule over you."

To Adam he said, "Because you listened to your wife and ate from the tree about which I commanded you, 'You must not eat of it,'

"Cursed is the ground because of you;
through painful toil you will eat
of it
all the days of your life.
It will produce thorns and thistles for
you,
and you will eat the plants of the
field.
By the sweat of your brow
you will eat your food
until you return to the ground,
since from it you were taken;
for dust you are
and to dust you will return."

Adam named his wife Eve, because she would become the mother of all the living.

The Lord God made garments of skin for Adam and his wife and clothed them. And the Lord God said, "The man has now become like one of us, knowing good and evil. He must not be allowed to reach out his hand and take also from the tree of life and eat, and live forever." So the Lord God banished him from the Garden of Eden to work the ground from which he had been taken. After he drove the man out, he placed on the east side of the Garden of Eden cherubim and a flaming sword flashing back and forth to guard the way to the tree of life.

Final Note: Eve's story is recorded in Genesis 2:19–4:25. (There are two references to Eve in the New Testament.) The Genesis account was written for the people of Israel by Moses, some time between 1470–1450 BC. Its purpose was "to record God's creation of the world and his desire to have a people set apart to worship him."[7]

Multicolored Jealousy

A Story about Family Dysfunction and Betrayal

Coming in the door with my arms full of groceries I heard a scream followed by a quick succession of angry demands. It was my sixteen-year-old daughter's voice.

"Get out! Don't you come one step closer! Get away from me!"

Dropping the grocery bags, I grabbed the portable phone and raced up the stairs two at a time to rescue Amber Joy from the unknown assailant. I had no weapon but was ready to clobber the enemy over the head with the phone and then call 911. Arriving at the scene of the crime, I discovered that the villain who had dared to step within Amber's room was her twelve-year-old brother.

True: Josh was armed with a loaded Nerf toy gun. True: He had sneaked in and swiped Pippi, our pet cat, who had been sleeping peacefully at the end of her bed. True: Upon Amber's irate objection, he had shot her in the arm with a yellow sponge ball. False: Her life had been in danger. True: She couldn't stand her brother, and he couldn't stand her!

My husband and I had two strong-willed children, and for years, sibling rivalry raged in our fine Christian home. Amber didn't want her brother anywhere near her personal space, her friends, or her things. But the meaner she got, the bolder he became.

They shared a bathroom, and to Josh's disgust, he was neat and Amber was not. He painstakingly wrote out a list of "bathroom etiquette" they should both follow, listing things like:

1. Wash your own toothpaste splatters off the mirror!
2. After washing your hair, de-clog tub drain of all accumulated hair!
3. Do not leave your disgusting retainer on the bathroom counter!
4. Keep all female sanitary products out of my sight. At this point, I do not care to further my knowledge of the facts of life!

When she transgressed, he retaliated. When he was obnoxious, she was rude in return. As parents, we mediated disputes, set and maintained guidelines and rules, and offered counsel and discipline. It is true that there were occasional times of happy family interaction. But to be honest, our favorite times with our children during those years of conflict were not the family vacations when we were all together, smiling for the pictures. They were the weeks when one child was gone to music or soccer camp, and we had the other at home alone.

Maturity brought an end to the war. As of this writing, Josh is a university student and Amber is a public school teacher. For several years now, the two former enemies have been close friends, talking on the phone each week, often for more than an hour at a time. They share a love for the piano, the theater, classic Nintendo, politics, and God. They discuss their social lives and ask for and value the advice of the other. This past December, Josh flew to Baltimore to visit Amber's inner-city classroom and to drive with her back to Michigan for the holidays, just so they could have some time together. When I remember their stormy past, their relationship today seems almost impossible. It is an answer to their parents' prayers. Miracles do happen!

SIBLING RIVALRY has disturbed the peace in homes throughout time, often leaving brothers and sisters with humorous tales about growing up to relate to their own children a generation later. However, if that rivalry is allowed to become abusive, there is nothing funny about it.

A chilling story in Scripture tells about a family that was so eaten up with jealousy and hate that the older brothers in the family literally plotted the death of their younger half brother. The boy was Joseph, the eleventh son of Jacob.

Joseph's Youth

Opening his eyes, seventeen-year-old Joseph stared up at the star-studded sky. For a moment he thought he was still dreaming, but the breeze that ruffled his hair was real enough, as was the sound of snoring coming from a nearby tent. Hearing the noise reminded him of his half brothers, and a long sigh escaped him. When he had told them about his first dream, in which his sheaf of grain had stood straight up and all of theirs had bowed before it, they had been angry. He could still hear their mocking insults and could imagine how displeased they would be about this new dream.

He loved his big family and accepted its uniqueness without question. His father, Jacob, the revered leader of their clan, had married two women—Leah, who gave birth to six sons and a daughter, and her beautiful sister, Rachel, who was Joseph's mother. In addition, Jacob had two concubines, Bilhah and Zilpah, who had two sons each. As one of the youngest in the family and greatly loved by his father, Joseph was secure enough not to be overly disturbed by the criticism of his ten older brothers.

Feeling the breeze pick up, Joseph wrapped his coat more tightly around himself, burying his chin within its folds. That was another irritation to his brothers. His coat. In the darkness its vibrant colors were muted, but in the daylight it was stunning. When his father had presented the beautiful garment to him, his brothers had watched in stony, jealous silence, but once their father was out of hearing, the taunts had begun.

"Here comes the peacock. Aren't you overdressed for shepherding? Stop! You'll blind the sheep." But what started in jest often ended in ridicule. "Go back to your mama, little boy. You might get your pretty coat dirty!"

Dan, Naphtali, Gad, and Asher, the sons of Jacob's concubines, were especially harsh. Some time before, Joseph had witnessed misconduct on their part and reported it to their father. They had never forgotten it. "Get out of here, you pampered snitch. Go spy on a snake and get yourself bitten!"

Oh well, Joseph thought optimistically. *I'm just too young for them to appreciate, but soon I will prove myself useful to my brothers and earn their respect.*

THAT THOUGHT SEEMED foolish the following evening when he told his brothers about his latest dream.

"God gave me another message in the form of a dream," Joseph began. There were several snorts and an audible groan from around the circle as he continued. "Listen," he insisted. "This time the sun and moon and eleven stars were bowing down to me."

"If you think that means we will ever bow before you, you'd better think again, Joseph," Reuben, his oldest brother, said as he rose to leave for his own tent. "It might be wise for you to remember that you are not the firstborn."

At Reuben's exit the others spat on the ground and took their own leave.

WEEKS LATER, Jacob called Joseph to him. *What a fine son! He has my intelligence and his mother's beauty,* he thought proudly. "Come here, my son," he said, patting the place beside him. "Your brothers have taken my flocks to graze near Shechem. I am going to send you to them to see if all is well, and I want you to bring word back to me."

"I will do that, Father," Joseph replied obediently. Although his brothers never seemed anxious to see him, surely they would want word of their home and families—and besides, it would be an adventure.

IT WAS NO SMALL journey to find his brothers, but Joseph didn't mind. He was pleased that his father would send him on a man's errand rather than keep him at home like a boy. And it was pleasant to have some time alone—Joseph was part of a large family unit, so the opportunity to be truly alone was rare.

The trip to Shechem was more than fifty miles; the journey gave him time to think about the strange dreams he had been having and to wonder at what God was saying to him.

When he arrived at Shechem, his brothers were not there. At first, he wandered over one hill and then another, thinking that surely they would be over the next rise. But his worry and frustration only grew. He was finally spotted by a local who told Joseph that he had met up with his brothers earlier, and that they had talked about going on to Dothan, about forty miles farther. Extremely relieved, Joseph headed out once again.

When he finally saw his brothers and their flocks in the distance, he was overjoyed. Waving his arms in the air, he hurried toward them as fast as his weary body could carry him.

JOSEPH WAS STILL quite far away when Reuben spotted him and alerted the others. In the late morning sun, the colors of Joseph's coat easily identified him despite the distance.

"Here comes the dreamer," he said.

"Looking like a peacock and flapping his wings like a chicken," said another. "Look how he hurries to be with his loving brothers!" Sarcastic laughter erupted in the group.

"He's no doubt here to poke into our business and then to go squawking back to our father," Asher said. "I'd like to wring his scrawny neck and pluck his feathers."

"So let's do it," Napthali replied. His comment was met with bitter laughter. "I mean it. Let's kill him. We can throw his body into one of these dry cisterns and say that a wild animal devoured him."

There was silence for a few moments before Simeon spoke up. "He does have such favor with our father that he's a threat to our own inheritances," he said thoughtfully. "It is true that we would be rid of our nemesis."

"Then we are agreed!" Napthali declared for all of them. Then he laughed as Joseph approached. "Look how the lamb hurries to his slaughter."

"Wait!" said Reuben, who knew he was already out of favor with his father for a great sin he had committed. Since he was the eldest, the blame would surely fall on his head if they were found out. "Let's not kill him ourselves. I propose we throw him in the cistern but that we don't harm him. He'll die of hunger or thirst, and we won't have his blood on our own hands. He's almost here. Are we agreed?"

"Hello!" Joseph called out, waving excitedly as he neared his brothers. "I've walked for days to find you!" Thirsty and breathless he joined the group, too relieved at finally having found them to be alarmed by their lack of greeting.

"Now!" Gad yelled.

Shock ran through Joseph as his brothers leaped upon him. "Get the coat!" Napthali urged.

Joseph felt the garment being wrenched away from him. "What's going on?" he asked in confusion. His brothers didn't respond; they only lifted him up, carried him a short way, and dropped him into a deep hole in the ground.

The few seconds it took to reach the bottom were painful as his back, legs, and arms scraped against the sides of the deep cistern. After landing hard, he felt shaken, bruised, and out of breath, but he soon determined that no bones had been broken. Getting to his feet, he strained to look above him to the opening in the ground. Several heads were silhouetted in the opening, but the faces were dark.

"Sweet dreams, little brother," someone called. Then there was laughter, and the faces were gone.

"Wait! Is this a joke?" Joseph yelled. "What's going on? Hey, come back! Let me out!"

Panic was setting in, and in the darkness Joseph felt the sides of the cistern, frantically feeling for a foothold to give him some leverage to climb out. *How deep is this pit?* he wondered. *Thirty, maybe forty feet deep?*

"Napthali!" he yelled, appealing to the brother closest to his age. "Napthali! Where are you?" When he received no answer, he appealed to others. "Judah! Levi! Dan! Issachar!" he yelled. "Help me! Please help me!"

His pleas went unanswered, and soon his dry, parched throat was aching for relief. His fingers and toes were scraped and bloody from trying in vain to climb out of the cistern.

Furious now, his cry changed. "Our father will be very angry over this!" he croaked. "He will punish you!" Unable to speak another word, he sank to the cold, gritty floor of the cistern and closed his eyes. He was exhausted. In the silence he heard a sound coming from above. It was laughter.

A horrible realization crept over Joseph as he leaned wearily against the wall of the cistern. This was no joke. His brothers truly hated him, and he would die here. Awareness of their betrayal brought with it a sickening sense of loss and disillusionment. Then, at the thought of never seeing his father again, he dropped his forehead against his upraised knees and wept.

Physically and emotionally spent, he cried out to his heavenly Father. "Oh, God, please help me." Then, utterly exhausted, he fell asleep.

ABOVE GROUND, the brothers ate lunch while passing around congratulations. But Reuben, increasingly uneasy over what had taken place, excused himself to check on the herd.

His mind was racing with a plan. He would leave with his brothers and then double back and rescue Joseph, but not before Joseph swore an oath that he would never tell what had transpired. The thought of Jacob's wrath chilled Reuben's blood as he recalled his father's anger at finding out that Reuben had slept with Bilhah, Jacob's concubine. He dared not risk his father's discovery of an even greater offense, or he would surely die. Satisfied with his plan, he headed back to his brothers.

JUDAH THOUGHTFULLY watched Reuben walk away from the group. As he turned back toward his brothers, Judah noticed a caravan approaching from the direction of Gilead. Since Dothan was along a major trade route to Egypt, this was not an uncommon sight, but as Judah watched its approach, an idea formed in his mind.

The Ishmaelites leading the caravan were indeed headed for Egypt, their camels loaded with spices, balm, and myrrh. From the look of things, they were also slave traders; several weary souls were chained together and straggling along behind the camels.

Brushing crumbs of bread from his full beard, Judah spoke up. "Listen, my brothers. What will we gain if we kill Joseph and cover up his blood? He is our brother, after all. Why don't we sell him to the slave traders approaching? The matter will then be out of our hands."

Asher laughed. "Good idea. Not only that, but we'll make some money on the deal!"

JOSEPH AWOKE to the sound of someone calling his name. Hope sprang in his heart as he recognized the voices of his brothers and saw a rope lowering toward him. A voice instructed him to tie it around himself so they could pull him out. His scraped knuckles were swollen and his fingers clumsy as he felt for the rope and awkwardly tied it around his body.

"I'm ready," his voice rasped through his parched throat. Then, grasping the rope between his hands and bracing his feet against the side of the cistern as best he could, he began his ascent. When he neared the top, strong arms reached down to haul him up and out.

Joseph was temporarily blinded by the brightness of the day; he reached up his hand to shield his face. "I thought you were going to abandon me," he whispered hoarsely.

Levi removed the rope from his waist, but in the next moment Dan grabbed his hands and bound his wrists.

"What are you doing?" Joseph asked in confusion. Then, with his vision clearing, he saw the caravan for the first time. Judah and Simeon stood together talking to a man obviously in charge. They gestured toward him, and once again Joseph was overwhelmed with the realization that he had been betrayed by his own flesh and blood.

He stood there looking from one brother to another with his undergarment stained and torn and his face dirty and tear streaked. Some were enjoying his misery. Others had the grace to look away.

His new "owner" approached and reached for Joseph's jaw and forced his mouth open. Running a filthy finger over Joseph's gums, the man checked his teeth and then gave an order for one of Joseph's ankles to be shackled. Then Joseph was attached by a length of chain to the slave ahead of him.

Humiliated and hopeless, he looked back only once to see money passing to the hands of his brothers. He wondered fleetingly how much the sale of a rich man's son was worth. The purchase price was twenty shekels, or about eight ounces of silver.[1]

WITH HIS PLAN for rescuing Joseph in mind, Reuben returned to his brothers in better spirits than when he had left. Upon arriving, he found them celebrating and bragging about the deal they had made with the slave traders.

"Reuben, we have two coins for you. Come get your share of the bounty!"

"What have you done?" Frantic, Reuben ran to the cistern, calling for Joseph, hoping that this was just another cruel joke. But the reality was that Joseph was gone. Terrified for himself, Reuben tore his clothes. Rushing back to his brothers, he said, "The boy isn't there! Where can I turn now?"

The seriousness of facing their father without Joseph called for another family meeting—they decided they would kill a goat, dip Joseph's coat in the blood, and present it to their father, saying that they had found the robe on their way home.

THEY WENT BEFORE Jacob as a group and laid the garment before him. "Do you recognize this robe? Examine it to see whether it is your son's," they said to him.

Jacob reached a trembling hand and touched the ornamentation on the robe he knew so well. He began weeping. "This is Joseph's robe! He has surely been torn to pieces by some ferocious animal." In anguish, Jacob tore his own clothes and mourned for his son for many days. Even though all of his children came to comfort him, he refused to be comforted. He wept bitterly for Joseph, saying, "I will go to my grave grieving for my son."

JOSEPH'S TREK into Egypt took about thirty days[2] and led him across the desert and far from familiar territory. It was a journey of grief as he relived the hatred and betrayal of his brothers and came to realize that his life would never be the same.

Once Joseph arrived at the great civilization of Egypt, another lesson in humility awaited him. Instructed to wash, Joseph was given a skirt of sorts that wrapped around his waist and left his chest bare. When led to the auction block, he was instructed to turn around several times. He clenched his teeth when men reached out to squeeze his calf muscles, testing his strength as they would an animal's. Buyers called out bids that he couldn't understand, and then the auctioneer gave an abrupt shout. Joseph, beloved son of Jacob, was sold. His new owner was Potiphar, one of Pharaoh's chief officials and the captain of the royal guard.

WE PAUSE HERE with Joseph being led away from the auction block. As hopeless as things seemed, Scripture goes on to tell us that God was with Joseph in all that he did. The next two chapters of this book will explore how, in many ways, Joseph's trials had only begun. However, great blessing was in store for him as God used the most difficult times in his life to prepare him for greatness.

Digging Deeper

Today we live in an age when blended families and sibling rivalry are commonplace, so Joseph's "blended family" experience is somewhat understandable to us. Sadly, however, Joseph also experienced a dysfunctional family unit and abusive brothers. As I studied this story, which took place in a culture so far removed from my own, questions kept coming to mind that needed answering. Dig a little deeper with me to better understand Joseph's situation and how we can apply this ancient story to our lives today.

What made up the family unit during Joseph's time? Today we have what is often referred to as a "nuclear" family—a small family with a mom, dad, and perhaps two or three children. This was not the case in Joseph's time. Ralph Gower, in his book *The New Manners and Customs of Bible Times*, gives us this information:

> Family units in Old Testament times were large and included every member of the family—aunts, uncles, cousins and servants. . . . The leader of the family was the father, and the head of a group of families was the shiekh. . . . Land passed from father to sons, the eldest son receiving twice as much as each of his brothers.
>
> The family was therefore a "little kingdom" that was ruled by the father. . . . Children were brought up to accept this authority (Exod. 20:12) and if they refused to accept it, thereby threatening the security of the family unit, they could be punished by death.[3]

In Joseph's situation, his father, Jacob, was the shiekh. Jacob had married two women who were sisters. He actually intended to marry only Rachel, Joseph's mother, and he worked for her father for seven years to earn that right. But his father-in-law, Laban, tricked him on his wedding night and literally switched the brides under the veil, marrying him off instead to Leah, Rachel's older sister. Jacob was furious, but the deed was done, so he agreed to work another seven years to get the bride he really loved. This fascinating story is found in Genesis 29–30, and it includes the story of how Jacob ended up fathering additional children by two concubines, who were also part of this blended family unit. When Rachel, who was much loved but devastated by her barrenness, finally gave birth to Joseph, the child became his father's favorite. (Rachel later gave birth to one more son, Benjamin.) Joseph's ten older brothers felt threatened by the favor their father showed Joseph, and despised him for it. The long and short of it is there was terrible rivalry between the wives and children in this large extended family. Relationships were skewed, and Joseph, a very special child of God, not only grew up in the middle of it but also suffered as a victim of domestic violence.

It is interesting to note that in thinking they had ruined any chance for Joseph's dreams to come true, his brothers actually had put into action the very means that would allow those dreams to come to fruition. Joseph's story gives proof to the biblical claim that God truly can work anything together for good (Rom. 8:28).

What was the significance of the multicolored coat Jacob gave to Joseph? I had always assumed Joseph's brothers were simply jealous that he was given a nicer coat than they had. With deeper study I learned that both the coat and their resentment were far more complicated.

In Genesis 37:32, when the brothers produce the blood-stained robe for Jacob's examination, it is described as an "ornamented robe." The Life Application Bible notes that "Joseph's robe was probably the kind worn by royalty—long sleeved, ankle length and colorful."[4] Gower suggests that since "Rachel was always intended to be his first wife, therefore it was her elder son, Joseph, who became Jacob's heir and was given the distinctive coat to show it, even though he was born long after his stepbrothers."[5]

If that was the case, when his brothers saw Joseph receive that particular robe, they must have realized he would be the heir who would receive the double portion of the inheritance. Their father's action angered them, and they took their jealousy and resentment out on Joseph.

Why did Joseph tell his brothers about his dreams? It was interesting to note the multitude of references to Joseph as an immature braggart and certainly no diplomat during this stage of his life. If he realized his brothers were already angry that he had received the "royal" coat, it would have made sense to keep his mouth shut about the dreams. Right?

I would like to present a different perspective. I believe God *compelled* him to share his dreams, not only with his brothers but also with his father. Of course, it is possible that Joseph enjoyed irritating his brothers by relaying the dreams, or that in his excitement and immaturity he said more than was necessary. Perhaps his presentation skills were those of a teenager lacking tact, but I believe he *had* to tell them. God wanted Joseph's family to know about the dreams. In the first dream, only his brothers bowed before him, but in the second, his father also bowed. This irritated even Jacob to hear it, and he rebuked Joseph in Genesis 37:10. But the eleventh verse says that even though his brothers went away mad, his father kept the matter in mind. (Jacob had experienced some pretty incredible dreams in his own past and couldn't simply dismiss the matter.)

In actuality, his brothers one day did bow before him. They later went back to get their father, and then all of them bowed (Genesis 42–46). I would like to suggest that God caused Joseph to relay the dreams to his family because they were prophetic messages of what would come. When the dreams came true, his family needed to recognize it was God who had brought them to that point in time.

So what *is* a cistern? This story took place in an arid land where there was little rain during at least half the year. The "pit" where Joseph was thrown was a dry cistern. Usually dug out of limestone, cisterns were used for water storage. "A cistern differs from a well in that a well is fed by underground water seepage, while a cistern stores runoff rainwater."[6] We are not told if this particular cistern was dry because it had cracked and therefore had become ineffective or because it was the dry season.

We know that Joseph was unable to get out by himself, but just how deep was the pit? That detail isn't given to us, but I did a little research and found references to several excavated cisterns that were fifty-five and sixty feet deep![7]

Were all the brothers in on the assault? A gang of ten grown men? It certainly sounds like they all collaborated. We later learn that Reuben had second thoughts (as self-preserving as they were), and that Judah led the change in plans to sell Joseph as a slave rather than be responsible for his eventual death in the pit. I found myself wondering if they all attacked him (which seems unlikely or unnecessary to subdue one boy) or if some of the brothers were bystanders who simply stood by and allowed the atrocities to take place. However active or passive their role, they were all guilty.

How can this story apply to your life?

Be a fair, loving, and observant parent. If you are a parent, ask yourself the following questions (and if you're not, reflect on how your parents raised you): Do I know where my children are at any given time? Do I know what they are doing? Do I show favoritism that may build up one child but discourage another? Do I firmly but lovingly set guidelines and boundaries for my children? Is there a filter on the family computer that will block out pornographic or violent material? Have I ever allowed one child to physically or emotionally hurt another? Have I been aware of abuse but done nothing to stop it?

Throughout Joseph's story, I found myself wondering what planet Jacob was on. How could he miss the animosity between his sons? He might have felt justified in making Joseph his heir, but he obviously did not feel it was necessary to assure his older sons that he would treat them fairly. But before I give Jacob too harsh a review, I have to admit that the spiritual training young Joseph received at home must have been good, because when he was separated from his family and living in a faraway pagan land, he stayed true to the faith of his father and honored God with his life.

Joseph was called the son of his father's old age, and by the time he was born, Jacob's older sons were tending to the family business and minding the flocks. Perhaps in semi-retirement, Jacob had more time to spend with young Joseph than he had to spend with his older sons when they were children. He was probably a better father to Joseph than he had been to the older boys, if their behavior is any indication of their upbringing.

Whatever your age or the age of your children, resolve to be fair, loving, and observant. If you are raising young children, don't get so caught up in your own interests that you neglect their emotional, physical, and spiritual well-being—and never allow a child to be abused!

A young man told me that he was the youngest of four boys in his family, and he had one brother in particular who constantly picked on him. His mother was an at-home mom, but she kept track of his dad's appointments and did the bookkeeping for his business. "She was always on the phone. I rarely felt like she was available to save me from my abusive brother," he said. "She was too busy to deal with us."

Sadder yet was the childhood of a female friend who was sexually abused by her father. Although her mother was aware of what was happening, she never intervened. "I was abused by my father and betrayed by my mother," my friend wept. "He hurt me, and she should have protected me."

Here is one last comment on being a fair, loving, and observant parent. When it comes time to write your last will and testament, please be fair and loving with your children. This is the last personal message you will leave your family. My husband, a probate and family court judge, can tell horror stories about the family strife parents leave behind when they do not treat their children fairly. Your last "testament" can leave a loving affirmation or it can breed discord and bitterness among your children.

If you identify with Joseph in this story, take heart. God loved Joseph and had a plan for his life that could not be deterred by the evil plans of others. Although Joseph endured intolerable injustice, he was able to somehow deal with that suffering. "One thing he did to cope with the pain was to . . . look back on it from the perspective of, *What was God's purpose in all of this?*"[8] Joseph later would tell his brothers, "You intended to harm me, but God intended it for good" (Gen. 50:20).

I have no doubt that some people reading this chapter have suffered abuse by a family member or others. Be encouraged by the fact that although it may look as though all is lost within the context of this one episode of Joseph's life, Joseph comes out an amazing winner! He honored God by living a life of integrity with spiritual perspective. In spite of years of slavery, abuse, and imprisonment, he knew God was with him in all that he did. God used the worst times in Joseph's life to prepare him for greatness beyond his wildest dreams.

Where should you begin? Take comfort in God's love for you, and when facing a painful situation, remember that "the beginning of a Joseph-like attitude is to acknowledge that God is with you. There is nothing like his presence to shed new light on a dark situation."[9]

In thinking about the emotions Joseph must have experienced during this horrific episode in his life, I realize he must have experienced shock, terror, desperation, humiliation, disillusionment, and perhaps even hopelessness. I found myself reflecting on an incident in my own life that was accompanied by these same emotions.

NEARING MY DESTINATION, I noted with satisfaction that the clock on the dash indicated I was fifteen minutes early for class.

"Perfect," I said out loud as I drove past the university building where my class would start at 6:00 p.m. I turned into a nearby mall parking lot and parked near the entrance to the food court so I could run in and order a large Pepsi on ice to help keep me alert during my four-hour class.

Emerging from the mall minutes later, I headed for my vehicle. I unlocked the car and set the drink in the holder before getting in. The thundering footsteps behind me were unexpected, and I was suddenly shoved hard against the car.

"Give me the keys!"

"Whaaaat?" With my heart racing, I craned my neck around to see my assailant. I was shocked to see a stocky young woman.

"I will not!" I said indignantly. I was both stunned and angered. Throwing my keys and purse onto the floor on the passenger side, I attempted to get in the car. She grabbed my shoulder, wrenched me back out, and shoved me hard against the vehicle. Grabbing the front of my coat in her fist, she put her face up to mine.

"Then you're going to take me for a ride, aren't you?" she growled.

As I looked into that malevolent face and felt her breath on my own, I experienced heart-pounding fear. Up so close, I was aware that her neck was severely scarred and purplish in color, which added to her bizarre and frightening demeanor. I believed she could kill me.

My mouth opened in desperate response to the sense of evil I felt around me.

"In the name of Jesus, let go of me!"

Those words seemed to startle her, and to my surprise, she released my coat but kept me trapped in the space between the door and the frame of the vehicle, with her body pushed against mine. Then, from the corner of my eye, I saw several people getting out of their cars on my right. I started screaming.

"Help me! Please help me! I'm being assaulted!"

In the distance, people paused for a moment but then turned away. Some seemed curious, but no one was willing to get involved. My desperation rose as an older couple approached, lowered their eyes, and turned away.

"Oh, please don't leave!" I begged them, sincerely believing that as long as there were witnesses, this crazy woman who had trapped me would not hurt me further or continue with my abduction. "Please don't leave!"

The menacing voice jeered in my face. "There they go, and just look how scared to death you are."

I realized for the first time that I was trembling violently. Her mockery made me angry, but my anger did nothing to stop the involuntary shaking. Then I saw a young woman cautiously approaching from my left.

"What's going on here?" she asked.

"Please help—" I started to say, only to be loudly interrupted by my assailant.

"This woman stole my parents' car and refuses to give me the keys!" my tormentor shouted.

"That's not what it looks like to me," the witness said. "As I was parking my car, I saw you attack this woman. I saw you push her, and I saw you yank her out of her car when she tried to get in. I'm not leaving here until you release her!"

My captor raised her voice several decibels. "She stole this car from the airport parking lot this morning!" She reached down and started digging in the side pocket of my door, pulling maps and miscellaneous papers out and claiming that this item and that item belonged to her parents.

I looked at her incredulously. Could she possibly believe that what she was saying was true, or was she just making this up to get rid of the bystanders? While she carried on loudly to a few curious men passing by, I made frantic eye contact with the witness, and my words spilled out on top of each other.

"Oh, thank you for staying! Thank you! Could you please get my purse from the floor on the passenger side? There's a cell phone in it. Call the police! My name is Jennie Dimkoff, I have identification in the glove box. I swear this is my vehicle. Oh, thank you for helping me!"

The witness's name was Kim, and she phoned the police. In fact, she called them three times before they actually arrived. My assailant became in-my-face aggressive while we waited, and Kim tried to distract her. She comforted me more than once with her words. "You'll be free soon. Just hang on. The police will be here soon."

Thinking back on that evening still isn't easy. It isn't pleasant to recall the harsh demands of my assailant, the violent pounding of my heart, the smell of my own fear-induced perspiration, or later, the pain from multiple contusions on my left arm and shoulder. Worst of all was remembering the hopeless despair I'd felt, realizing that men and women walking by were not going to help me. It was one of the most demoralizing events of my lifetime. It shook my faith in humankind.

But Kim showed pure, unselfish altruism to me. She was a lifeline. She gave me hope. After the police arrived, I burst into tears, and she gave her statement. Before we parted I got her phone number and said I would like to take her for lunch sometime, and she agreed.

59

We spoke on the phone several times after that, but it was not until that lunch date, more than a month later, that I learned Kim had indeed spontaneously sacrificed for me. In our conversation over lunch, she mentioned that she had epilepsy and had suffered for years with an anxiety disorder that sometimes triggered grand mal seizures. I was stunned.

"Kim, are you telling me that you helped me in spite of the fact that the stress of that bizarre situation could have caused you to have a seizure?"

"That's right," she answered. "Isn't it great that I didn't have one? I heard you call out 'In Jesus' name, let go of me,' and I just couldn't walk away."

"Kim, before we leave today, I have a little gift for you. It's a book I really like about finding hope and even humor in unexpected places. I'd also like to tell you something that's very important to me. I'm a Christian, and I believe that God prompted you to help me and that he protected both of us through that crisis. I couldn't meet you today without telling you that I've been praying for you ever since that night."

We both had tears in our eyes, and we hugged as we said good-bye.

A few weeks later a priceless email arrived from Kim.

> *Hi Jennie: I've never been much of a reader, but I've read the book you gave me from cover to cover. I've made a lot of mistakes in my life, and even though I was raised to know God, I've made some choices that have taken me far away from a right relationship with him. Jennie, I know that you think that God brought me into your life that night in the parking lot to help you, but I believe that he connected us there so you could remind me how much I needed to make my life right with him. Thank you for helping me to see that.*
>
> *From your friend, Kim*

I read Kim's email several times that day, considering what she had written. I would never have chosen the circumstances of that evening, but I came to realize that what someone else meant for evil, God used for good.

A Whispered Prayer

Dear Heavenly Father, thank you for my family. We're imperfect, Lord, but I believe you can use even our mistakes to teach us lessons we need to learn. Where I have been wronged, please give me a heart of forgiveness, and help me to trust you to bring good out of even those situations. And where I have failed, Lord, please forgive me and help me to be the wife, mother, daughter, sister, or friend you would have me be. In the precious name of Jesus, Amen.

Get Up and Go Ideas for Tomorrow

1. I will pray for my children's physical, emotional, and spiritual well-being, asking God to reveal to me how I can be a better parent to them.
2. I will call up my sister(s) or brother(s) and tell them that I love them. If I remember giving them a hard time when we were growing up, I will apologize.
3. I will encourage someone in distress today. (This could be ordering a pizza for a stressed-out college student, phoning

911 for someone you pass on the highway, or baby-sitting for a new mother, to give just a few ideas.)

A Thought to Ponder as I Fall Asleep

When was the last time I told my parents, my children, and/or my siblings that I love them?

The Scripture Reading: Genesis 37:1–36

Jacob lived in the land where his father had stayed, the land of Canaan.

This is the account of Jacob.

Joseph, a young man of seventeen, was tending the flocks with his brothers, the sons of Bilhah and the sons of Zilpah, his father's wives, and he brought their father a bad report about them.

Now Israel loved Joseph more than any of his other sons, because he had been born to him in his old age; and he made a richly ornamented robe for him. When his brothers saw that their father loved him more than any of them, they hated him and could not speak a kind word to him.

Joseph had a dream, and when he told it to his brothers, they hated him all the more. He said to them, "Listen to this dream I had: We were binding sheaves of grain out in the field when suddenly my sheaf rose and stood upright, while your sheaves gathered around mine and bowed down to it."

His brothers said to him, "Do you intend to reign over us? Will you actually rule us?" And they hated him all the more because of his dream and what he had said.

Then he had another dream, and he told it to his brothers. "Listen," he said, "I had another dream, and this time the sun and moon and eleven stars were bowing down to me."

When he told his father as well as his brothers, his father rebuked him and said, "What is this dream you had? Will your mother and I and your brothers actually come and bow down to the ground before you?" His brothers were jealous of him, but his father kept the matter in mind.

Now his brothers had gone to graze their father's flocks near Shechem, and Israel said to Joseph, "As you know, your brothers are grazing the flocks near Shechem. Come, I am going to send you to them."

"Very well," he replied.

So he said to him, "Go and see if all is well with your brothers and with the flocks, and bring word back to me." Then he sent him off from the Valley of Hebron.

When Joseph arrived at Shechem, a man found him wandering around in the fields and asked him, "What are you looking for?"

He replied, "I'm looking for my brothers. Can you tell me where they are grazing their flocks?"

"They have moved on from here," the man answered. "I heard them say, 'Let's go to Dothan.'"

So Joseph went after his brothers and found them near Dothan. But they saw him in the distance, and before he reached them, they plotted to kill him.

"Here comes that dreamer!" they said to each other. "Come now, let's kill him and throw him into one of these cisterns and say that a ferocious animal devoured him. Then we'll see what comes of his dreams."

When Reuben heard this, he tried to rescue him from their hands. "Let's not take his life," he said. "Don't shed any blood. Throw him into this cistern here in the desert, but don't lay a hand on him." Reuben said this to rescue him from them and take him back to his father.

So when Joseph came to his brothers, they stripped him of his robe—the richly ornamented robe he was wearing—and they took him and threw him into the cistern. Now the cistern was empty; there was no water in it.

As they sat down to eat their meal, they looked up and saw a caravan of Ishmaelites coming from Gilead. Their camels were loaded with spices, balm and myrrh, and they were on their way to take them down to Egypt.

Judah said to his brothers, "What will we gain if we kill our brother and cover up his blood? Come, let's sell him to the Ishmaelites and not lay our hands on him; after all, he is our brother, our own flesh and blood." His brothers agreed.

So when the Midianite merchants came by, his brothers pulled Joseph up out of the cistern and sold him for twenty shekels of silver to the Ishmaelites, who took him to Egypt.

When Reuben returned to the cistern and saw that Joseph was not there, he tore his clothes. He went back to his brothers and said, "The boy isn't there! Where can I turn now?"

Then they got Joseph's robe, slaughtered a goat and dipped the robe in the blood. They took the ornamented robe back to their father and said, "We found this. Examine it to see whether it is your son's robe."

He recognized it and said, "It is my son's robe! Some ferocious animal has devoured him. Joseph has surely been torn to pieces."

Then Jacob tore his clothes, put on sackcloth and mourned for his son many days. All his sons and daughters came to comfort him, but he refused to be comforted. "No," he said, "in mourning will I go down to the grave to my son." So his father wept for him.

Meanwhile, the Midianites sold Joseph in Egypt to Potiphar, one of Pharaoh's officials, the captain of the guard.

Final Note: Genesis 12–50 "focuses on the lives of four patriarchs of the faith: Abraham, Isaac, Jacob, and Joseph, from whom will come the nation of Israel and ultimately the Savior, Jesus Christ."[10]

THREE

Good Guy, Bad Times

A Story about Bad Things That Happened to a Good Person

Sitting down on the floor in our living room, I found myself lost in the past as I studied eight or ten photo albums that lined the bottom shelf of the bookcase. While immersed in those photos that spanned about thirty years of family history, I realized that there were recurring themes recorded within the pages. We had chosen to preserve pictorial records of vacations, birthdays, weddings, family reunions, graduations, and so on. Not many ordinary days were recorded. Furthermore, if I could choose one word to describe how we had asked one another to pose for those memorable pictures, it would be "SMILE!" Why do you suppose we did that? Why, it's because we wanted to remember how happy we were!

Now, be honest. When was the last time you opened an album and saw a caption under a picture that read "This is Josh the day he struck out twice in Little League" or "This is our daughter, Amber, thrown across her bed weeping after she broke her first boyfriend's heart." How about this caption under a close-up on the next page: "Uncle Bud's mug shot," and a page later, "This is Grandma the day Grandpa died."

There are some days we'd just as soon forget.

It's interesting that we have an amazing "album" available to us that records the stories of hundreds of characters from history, in which not all the characters are recorded smiling. The Bible gives us the good, the bad, and the ugly. We find records of individuals who obeyed God and those who disobeyed. There are good times and hard times recorded, and stories of both joy and sorrow. Why do you think God gave us such a revealing glimpse into the past? In 2 Timothy 3:16–17 we are told that "all Scripture is God-breathed and is useful for teaching, rebuking, correcting and training in righteousness, so that the man [woman] of God may be thoroughly equipped for every good work." In other words, each story is included for a purpose, and there is something we can learn from it.

The early life of Joseph is one of those stories in which there seems little to smile about, like everything went wrong for a good person. But what is amazing to learn is that through it all, God was with Joseph. God protected him when others meant to harm or destroy him, and God used the hardest circumstances in his life to prepare him for moments of unimaginable greatness. Step back in time as we check in once again with Joseph as he labors as a slave in Egypt. As this episode in his life opens, he is working in the household of his owner, Potiphar, a military officer and captain of Pharaoh's guard. Now in his early twenties, Joseph is a capable and trusted servant.

Joseph's Servitude

Crossing the inner courtyard on his way to the stables, Joseph noted that the leafy palms growing from massive brick planters lining the walkway needed to be watered. Pausing a moment as his eyes swept the other vegetation, he made a mental note to have the gardener attend to the matter within the hour. The hot Egyptian sun had tanned his skin a warm brown, and as he bent to thrust a finger into a planter, he was unaware that someone was watching the play of the sun on the muscles of his back and shoulders with great interest.

The gardens in the courtyard were beautiful, but it was the agricultural center beyond the family compound that demanded more of Joseph's attention. Farming in Egypt was carried out with the utmost precision, and with the crops thriving, Joseph would soon arrange for the grain to be harvested.

Soon the master of the household appeared at an outer archway and approached Joseph with a purposeful stride. His normally stern face broke into a smile.

"Joseph! I have just come from the stables, and the new foal is faring very well. What a fine young stallion he will be. With your careful attention, my stable will be the envy of all Egypt!"

"I was just on my way to check on the foal and the mare myself," Joseph responded, grinning with genuine warmth at his master. It pleased Joseph greatly to see that God's hand of blessing had fallen on Potiphar since the day Potiphar had entrusted responsibility to him. The young slave had been as quick to learn the language as he had been to prove himself a faithful and trustworthy servant in the months and years that followed his purchase from the auction block. With each responsibility Potiphar had given Joseph, more financial gain had come back to Potiphar, and the master realized he had not earned this blessing himself.

"Do you know how good it feels to arrive home and not have to concern myself with anything except my beautiful wife and my dinner?" Potiphar asked with a laugh.

Warmed by Potiphar's words of approval, Joseph went on with his duties, comforted in the knowledge that even as a slave, he could earn the respect of others. This was not the position in life he would have selected had he been given a choice, but he gratefully acknowledged that he was in a place where he could learn valuable skills and exercise the intelligence God had given him.

Later that night, long after the wealthy household had retired, a restless Joseph got up and stepped out into the darkness to stare up at the star-filled sky. Breathing deeply of the cool night air, he studied the heavens and once again recalled the dreams of his youth in which the sun, moon, and stars had bowed down to him. Sighing deeply, he marveled at the difference between receiving a message from God and understanding how that message could ever come to fruition. Memories of how he had been uprooted from his family, sold as a slave, and taken as a confused young teenager to this household flooded his mind. Closing his eyes for a moment, he thanked God for never forsaking him and for bringing blessings to his master, Potiphar.

Joseph was so engrossed in his thoughts that he was startled when a cool hand touched his arm and trailed down to his elbow. Alarm shot through him as he recognized Potiphar's wife in the moonlight. "What is it, madam? Is my master well?"

"Relax, Joseph," the woman whispered with a slow smile. Reaching out again, she placed her hand on his chest and leaned closer. "I couldn't sleep and decided to get some air. I see we had the same idea."

But Joseph wasn't relaxed at all. Stepping back, he mumbled that if all was well, he was needed inside. After nodding his head awkwardly in her direction, he fled back to his own quarters.

Joseph heard her quiet laughter behind him as he slipped into his room.

IT BECAME A KIND of game for her. Watching. Stalking. Peeping. Seeking out Joseph and commanding him to meet some frivolous request that any of the other servants could have attended to. With Potiphar gone so much of the time, she had ample opportunity to observe her prey.

Joseph's discomfort amused her. The young slave had literally grown up in their household, and he was so attractive that just thinking of him made her mouth water. The fact that he never encouraged her advances both frustrated and intrigued her.

Spoiled, pampered, and jaded with life, Potiphar's wife didn't value the mutual respect her husband and Joseph had for each other, nor did she attribute the blessing that had come to their household to the work of Joseph. She thought only of herself.

At first it was enough simply to be a voyeur, but once she decided she would have Joseph sexually, the risk involved only added to the excitement. As mistress of the house, nothing was denied her, and she was determined to have Joseph in her bed. However, she knew Potiphar would be furious if he were to find out, so she would need to be careful.

IT WAS AWKWARD, fielding the advances of his master's wife. Joseph's position required that he treat her with the utmost respect and serve her as best he could, but things were getting ridiculous. As overseer of Potiphar's entire household and all of his business interests, Joseph had great authority, and although he had assigned others to meet her every need, his master's wife constantly seemed to require his personal attention.

At first she was subtle. She would suddenly appear in an area where he was working, always dressed in fine linen, her waist bound with an ornamented girdle, an intricately worked band of gold encircling her neck, and her eyes and brows darkly outlined with kohl. "It's fascinating to watch you work, Joseph," she would say. "I get so bored in the house all day."

Then she became bolder. "Come and walk to the goldfish pond with me, Joseph. I want to show you something." Upon reaching the pond, he would discover there was nothing that required his attention except his master's wife, and he would politely excuse himself. If she found him poring over records, she would lean against him, feigning interest in what he was doing, lightly brushing her breast against his arm or back. He would move away without being rude and ask what she required.

"Can't you guess, Joseph?" she finally responded one day, her painted lips coming together in a pout. "I require you. I desire you. Potiphar is away on business, and I require that you come to my bed. And believe me, Joseph, I'll make sure you enjoy every minute of our time together."

Faced with her overt directive, Joseph stammered, "I can't do that, madam." Then, trying to reason with her, he said, "My master has entrusted to my care all that he has, except you, his wife. It would be wicked to betray him and sin against God in such a way. I cannot do as you ask."

"Yes, you can, Joseph," his master's wife called after him as he walked away, "and you will."

Day after day, she beckoned to him, teased him, propositioned him, and day after day he refused her.

POTIPHAR WAS DUE back within a day, and Joseph was busy preparing a report of all business matters for his master's evaluation. He had reviewed the stables, the crops, and the grounds, and after meeting with the household staff, he would have his review completed. With a sigh, he set aside his writing instrument, grabbed his cloak, and headed for the main house. When no one answered his knock, he opened the door and stepped inside, surprised that there were no servants in attendance.

"Hello," he called out. "It's Joseph. Is anyone here?"

A door clicked behind him.

"Gotcha!" a woman's voice giggled. Turning slowly around, Joseph took in the sight of his master's wife. Leaning against the door with her gown slipping off one shoulder, she gave him a slow smile. "We're all alone, Joseph. I sent the servants away when you sent word that you were coming, and today is the day you *will* lie down with me."

Joseph swallowed hard and felt himself breaking out in a sweat. "You know I cannot, madam," he stated firmly, shaking his head. "It would be wrong."

She came toward him, reaching out to run her hands across his bare chest and over his shoulders to remove his coat. "Forget that conscience of yours, Joseph, and allow me to introduce you to a little carnal pleasure."

HIS REJECTION in recent days had eaten away at her pride. When he stubbornly didn't respond to her this time, she said, "I wanted this to be fun for both of us, Joseph, but you're starting to irritate me. Do I have to remind you of the fact you are a piece of property and I am the owner?" With that crude comment, she pushed his coat over his shoulder with one hand and reached up to encircle his neck with the other.

There was a slight struggle when he wrenched away from her. She had grabbed on to his coat, trying to pull him back, but he pulled his arms out of it to make his escape. The motion caused her to fall back, still clutching his coat in her hands.

Her attractive, painted face became ugly with hatred fueled by his rejection. "That was very foolish of you, Joseph," she hissed as he ran out the door and out of the house. Shaking with rage, she looked down at the coat in her hands. "I wonder how you will handle this!"

Reaching for her own garment, she tore at the fabric. After that, she started screaming.

When the household servants came running, they were shocked to find their mistress tearful, flushed, and angry. Waving Joseph's coat she said to them, "The Hebrew has tried to make sport of me in my husband's absence! He tried to come in here and sleep with me, but I screamed for help, and in his rush to get away, he left his cloak beside me!"

She kept her "evidence" next to her until her husband arrived home.

EXHAUSTED, HUNGRY, and eager for her company, Potiphar was shocked to find his beautiful wife weeping. Her face was streaked with black from dabbing at her kohl-lined eyes, and upon his arrival, she threw herself into his strong arms.

"What is it, my darling, my pet?" he asked anxiously, taking her by the shoulders so that he could look into her face.

"Oh, Potiphar! I wish you had been here," she wept. "That Hebrew slave that you brought here came to me to make sport of me! I was so afraid! But as soon as I screamed for help, he ran out of the house."

"What?" Potiphar roared, staring at her with disbelief. "That cannot be so! Joseph would never do such a thing."

"Well, he did," his wife said defensively, "and the servants all know about it!" Picking up the garment she had been guarding, she held it out triumphantly. "I've told you how your slave treated me, and here is proof. Not only was he here, he was undressing in my presence, and he left his coat behind." Throwing the garment at his feet, she covered her face with her hands and burst into another fit of weeping.

Potiphar stared at the familiar coat on the ground with shock for a moment before raising his eyes to the fragile, weeping figure of his wife. In slow motion he picked up the coat and turned it over in his hands. *I trusted Joseph. I gave him my own authority, and this is how he has repaid me.* Anger replaced shock, and as he stood there, anger turned to fury. Turning abruptly from his wife, he headed for the door. "I'll take care of Joseph. You'll never have to be afraid of a slave again."

Peeking at his retreating figure through her fingers, Potiphar's wife grinned with glee.

JOSEPH WAS A BIT shaken by the turn of events at the main house. Back at his own quarters, he was irritated to realize that he had left his coat behind. The woman would no doubt use the garment as an excuse to pester him the next time her husband's back was turned. With all the authority Potiphar had given him in this place, he was still a slave to be used and ordered about. The woman's crude reminder left him frustrated with being in such an impossible position. Should he say anything to Potiphar? He cringed at the thought. It would be his word against hers, and Joseph knew his master doted on his wife. Besides, he had no desire to cause Potiphar pain. With a heavy heart Joseph went back to preparing the quarterly report for his master's review.

SEVERAL HOURS LATER, Joseph was interrupted when the door burst open.

"Take him!"

Joseph looked up to find soldiers rushing in. In the next instant, his hands were bound. Shocked to see his master directing such an action, Joseph noticed his own coat balled up in Potiphar's hands.

"You Hebrew dog," Potiphar spat at him, shaking his head in disgust. "I trusted you with everything, only to be betrayed." Turning his back on Joseph, he ordered his men. "Take him to the prison."

As Joseph was roughly ushered out of the building and given over to the warden of the prison, a sickening realization came over him: Potiphar's wife had lied about him, and worst of all, Potiphar had believed her. The loss of his master's trust cut him like a knife.

That night as Joseph lay on the filthy floor of a crowded cell, despair washed over him. Once again it seemed his life had taken an unfair and frightening turn. Lifting his arm to cover his eyes and block out his surroundings, he turned his heart toward Jehovah God and cried out for help.

THE WARDEN'S EYES followed Joseph as he quietly moved around the cell area. By friendly words and his own example, the prisoner encouraged the others to clean up the squalid place. *Amazing. Potiphar's slave sticks out like a sore thumb,* the warden thought, *or perhaps he's more like a bright lamp in a very dark place.* The man had never seen anything like it. The young fellow seemed to have a natural ability to organize and lead. *Too bad more of the inmates I have to put up with aren't like that one,* he thought. *It sure would make my job easier.*

In the weeks and months that passed, Joseph's presence in the prison did indeed lighten the warden's responsibilities. God gave Joseph favor in the eyes of the warden, and Joseph was given first one responsibility and then another. Since the prison was located in the capital city, many who ended up incarcerated there were from wealthy backgrounds or from the royal court itself. Those used to privilege didn't take well to the squalor of the place, but Joseph's management made their situation better. Eventually, the warden had such confidence in Joseph that he made him the trustee, with the entire management of the prison coming under his authority.

PERIODICALLY, PRISONERS ARRIVED from Pharaoh's own household. Two such individuals who had fallen out of favor with their master were Pharaoh's baker and cupbearer. One morning Joseph was making his way throughout the prison, checking on each prisoner under his authority. When he came to the area where the king's baker and cupbearer were kept, he noticed that both of them seemed distressed. Concerned for their well-being, Joseph questioned them.

"Good morning, friends. I've never seen the two of you so down in the dumps before. Is there anything wrong beyond being here with the rest of us who wish we weren't here either?"

Obviously troubled, both men confessed that they had suffered from bad dreams the night before, dreams that no one seemed able to explain.

"Those interpretations belong to God," Joseph said. "He has revealed his secrets to me before; perhaps he will again. Tell me about the dreams."

The cupbearer began, saying that he had dreamed of a grapevine with three branches whose grapes he squeezed into Pharaoh's cup, and that he had handed the cup to Pharaoh.

Nodding with understanding, Joseph said, "This is what your dream means. In three days, Pharaoh will restore you to your position, and you will once again be placing his cup into his hand. Now, when this happens, mention me to Pharaoh and get me out of this prison. I've already been forcibly carried off from my homeland, and I have done nothing to deserve being placed in a dungeon. Don't forget me!"

Encouraged that the cupbearer had received such good news, the baker spoke up. "I dreamed that I had three baskets of bread on my head. The top basket had an assortment of breads for Pharaoh's table, but as I walked along, birds descended and began to eat the bread out of the basket. What could that strange dream mean?"

Exhaling, Joseph was quiet for a moment and then spoke. "Well, the three baskets once again mean three days," he began, "but on the third day, Pharaoh will hang you on a tree, and the birds will come and eat away at your flesh." An ominous quiet filled the room, and Joseph quietly left.

THREE DAYS LATER a feast was held in honor of Pharaoh's birthday. In front of his officials, Pharaoh called for his cupbearer and baker. As Joseph had predicted, the cupbearer was restored to his former position of honor, but the baker was hanged.

Once again the cupbearer placed the royal cup in Pharaoh's hand, and as the days, months, and then years went by, he forgot all about Joseph.

Digging Deeper

Joseph's life story reveals that his path to greatness was fraught with complications and mistreatment by others. But this chapter of More Night Whispers covers the final discouraging reports about Joseph. I'm relieved to tell you that only good things happen after this dark chapter in his life. In spite of the incredible challenges he faced, Joseph would survive and thrive!

Take a few minutes with me to look a little closer at this difficult period in Joseph's life and to find things we can apply to our own lives today.

How had Joseph's life changed with his circumstances? First, there was culture shock. The son of a nomadic shepherd was removed from his family and sold as a slave. Reeling from what had happened, he ended up in the wealthiest and most sophisticated city in the ancient world. In Egypt, there was great wealth and great poverty. Grand houses filled the city, and immense pyramids dotted the horizon. The Egyptians mummified their dead and worshiped idols. The language, dress, and grooming were different from what he was accustomed to. Every ritual was foreign to Joseph.

He was lost but not alone, because God was with him.

Joseph was sold to Potiphar, a royal officer in Pharaoh's army and captain of Pharaoh's guard. In All the Women of the Bible, Edith Deen describes a typical Egyptian royal house and the types of duties that were required of Joseph in that setting.

[The] house, similar to Egyptian royal houses of that period of about 1700 B.C., had a block of high rooms surrounding the main room and inner garden court.

This Egyptian house kept Joseph, the young overseer, busy, for it had stables and harness rooms, shelter for small wooden chariots, servant's quarters, granary courtyards, and conical grain bins, as well as an agricultural center. Even the trees, set in brick tubs containing Nile mud, had to be watered daily. There were slaves to direct, purchases to be made in the market, and distinguished guests who demanded personal attentions.[1]

Second, Joseph was given the tremendous responsibility of overseer, of which he proved himself worthy. The next big challenge came when he was sexually harassed by his master's wife.

Joseph literally grew into manhood in Potiphar's household, and the scriptural account tells us that he was one good-looking guy. In Genesis 39:6 it says, "Now Joseph was well-built and handsome, and after a while his master's wife took notice of Joseph."

Why didn't Joseph give in to Potiphar's wife? Talk about a tough work environment! Scripture says that Potiphar's wife harassed him to sleep with her every day! We aren't told how old she was or if Joseph was physically attracted to her in any way. What we do know is that he was a slave and therefore subject to the orders, and in this case the whims, of his owner. However, at this demand Joseph drew the line. Most in his position would have felt they had no choice.

So why did he refuse her? I agree with the *Baker Commentary on the Bible*, which points out that Joseph refused to become her lover for two reasons: "First, it would be a disservice to his master who has trusted him (30:8–9a). Second, it would be a sin against God (v. 9b). It is Joseph's commitment to high moral principle that keeps him free from an illicit affair."[2]

It is amazing to learn that although Joseph's circumstances changed drastically, his faith did not—especially when he worshiped God without other believers to encourage or mentor him. God was with him, and God gave him favor in the eyes of those in authority over him. I'm sure Joseph found favor in God's eyes as well. Uprooted from his former life, he stayed rooted in his faith and true to being a man of honesty and integrity.

Why was Joseph sent to prison rather than put to death? Attempted rape, the crime of which Joseph was accused, was punishable by death, and there seemed ample evidence against him. (Incidentally, isn't it interesting that this is the second time in Joseph's young life that his coat was used as evidence when others told a lie about him?) I'm sure that God's protection was upon Joseph, but it is interesting to speculate about why Potiphar put Joseph into prison rather than have him executed. Walter Elwell, who wrote the *Baker Commentary*, offers these questions: "Did Potiphar have reason to be suspicious of his wife's story? Had she done something like this before? Maybe Potiphar trusts Joseph more than he trusts his wife. If that is the case, caution is called for. You can release an innocent man from incarceration, but you cannot resurrect him."[3]

How was life in prison? Miserable. What made it even worse for Joseph is that he knew he didn't deserve to be there! We know he did not like being in prison because he asked Pharaoh's cupbearer to help get him out (Gen. 40:14)! The Life Application Bible offers some insight regarding what prison life was like for Joseph and the others incarcerated with him.

Prisons were grim places with vile conditions. They were used to house forced laborers or the accused who were awaiting trial, like Joseph. Prisoners were guilty until proven innocent, and there was no right to a speedy trial. Many prisoners never made it to court, because trials were held at the whim of the ruler.[4]

Once again we find that Joseph landed in a place he would not have chosen, and once again God was with him and gave him favor in the eyes of those in authority over him. Instead of becoming overwhelmed with depression and bitterness, Joseph kept doing his best and accepted new responsibility. How little did he realize that those years spent as a convict would be the last intense job-training session God would require of him before Pharaoh gave him the honor and responsibility of feeding the entire nation.

How can this story apply to your life?

Hold fast to your faith in the face of discouragement or persecution. Remember that God is with you and that he has called you according to his purpose (Rom. 8:28). Furthermore, he can use any experience for good in your life if you are open to his leading. Slavery, sexual harassment, and imprisonment were not Joseph's idea of a great life, but he kept true to his faith and honored God in everything he did. God not only helped him to survive those experiences, but he also used them to prepare Joseph to be the governor of Egypt.

Are you an on-the-job Christian? How is your work or ministry situation? Do you bring joy, order, compassion, and integrity to the workplace? Are you doing a menial task? Have you struggled with bitterness over being blamed for someone else's wrong-doing? Have you been frustrated with sexual harassment on the job? No matter what your circumstance is, God promises to be with you and not to forsake you (Heb. 13:5), but he wants you to behave with honesty and integrity. First Chronicles 29:17 says, "I know, my God, that you test the heart and are pleased with integrity."

Say no when confronted with an invitation to do something you know is wrong. Joseph stuck to his principles even when Potiphar's wife hounded him day after day. He didn't have the freedom to quit his job and remove himself from that awkward position, but you do! You do not have to be a slave to your employer or harasser. You can walk away and seek direction from God for a different place of employment.

If you have encountered sexual harassment, put an end to it! We are blessed today to have Christian counselors and lawyers, and laws that are there to protect individuals from such conduct.

- Pray for wisdom as you deal with the inappropriate behavior.
- Speak up and politely but firmly let the perpetrator know that his behavior offends you, or write him a letter expressing those thoughts (and keep a copy for your own records).
- Document (keep a journal or a tape recording, if possible) of each incident, just in case the situation escalates to a point that charges need to be filed or a personal protection order requested.
- Seek help. If the problem persists, speak to your supervisor, outline the situation for him or her, and ask for his or her recommendation. Keep a record of this meeting.
- If the problem escalates, remove yourself from any situation that has potential danger. Your job situation may be impossible, but thankfully, you have the freedom to leave.

You may think you can't get along without that particular job, but you can, and God may use this event in your life to open a more meaningful door of opportunity. And if you're feeling hurt over the anger or accusations of your tormentor, consider that that man's rejection may be God's protection.

Whew! How else can I apply Joseph's story to my life?
Pursue the dream or "calling" God lays on your heart. It may not be easy or convenient. It may require sacrifice and commitment, but God will be with you, and he will take great joy in completing the work he has begun in you.

From his youth, Joseph knew that God had a special plan for his life. Although he was the one in his family who would greatly succeed, the path that led to his success was an extraordinarily difficult and challenging one. Through every trial, he was faithful to God no matter what his circumstances, and he honored God with his life. It reminds me of the faithfulness of someone else.

MIKE AND CHER RIEPMA were young, vivacious, and excited about what God was accomplishing in their lives. They had just completed their first five-year term working with New Tribes Missions in a remote village located on a tributary of the Amazon River in Bolivia. My family met them while we were vacationing at Maranatha Bible and Missionary Conference Center on the shores of beautiful Lake Michigan.

The week started with Mike sharing how God had given him the dream of serving Christ in Bolivia. He met Cher, who was a nurse, while attending language school, and he was thrilled to discover that God had laid a passion for Bolivia on her heart as well! The daughter of New Tribes missionaries, Cher had grown up in Bolivia and had already completed both her nurse's training and the other New Tribes courses. Totally committed to God's call on her life, she left ahead of Mike to work as a nurse in the mission school at Tambo, Bolivia.

Mike longed to be with her and plodded doggedly ahead, but nothing about the adventure he was about to embark on was easy. While in the United States, Mike completed mission training, Bible school, language school, jungle training camp, and the important but difficult "deputation" that would raise the necessary funds to support their work, all the while believing that God would bring him and Cher together for a single purpose.

Living out of a suitcase, Mike began visiting churches, tirelessly sharing the vision God had given him for Bolivia and requesting consideration for support. Mike's family helped him pack the items he would need to survive and teach in a jungle for the next five years. Then, after a tearful good-bye to family and friends, Mike boarded an international flight that would take him to a new land, a precious love, and a new life.

The wedding ceremony took place in Bolivia a few months later. After a short honeymoon, Mike and Cher learned that it would take several days by boat to reach their assigned tribe. They threw themselves into getting their crates and footlockers on board and then settled in for a long boat ride on a winding, snake-infested river. It was the last leg of the journey that would lead them to the Ese Ejja tribe.

Their hearts were pounding with excitement as they rounded the last bend in the river. Up ahead they could see groups of natives gathered to watch the approaching boat. Totally committed to their cause, Mike and Cher felt they already loved the people they would come to live with, so it came as a rude surprise to discover that the native tribal people did not welcome them. With their arms across their chests, the men of the village observed Mike and Cher as they struggled to unload the small mountain of medical supplies and belongings. Exhausted, Mike thought to himself, *Well, they may not be excited about our coming, but I wish they would help with these crates!*

Their first home with the Ese Ejja was a humble, dirt floor structure ridden with cockroaches. Looking around in dismay, Cher bravely said, "It'll be a lot more homey when we get our wedding gifts unpacked and put some pictures on the walls."

Prying open the crates, they found that termites had gotten in ahead of them. While in storage, gifts from dear friends and precious memories of home had been ruined. After sadly sorting through the mess and making do with what was left, they fell into an exhausted sleep.

The days ahead were tough—discouraging and often lonely—but Mike and Cher Riepma never gave up. With stubborn faith they clung to the dream, the mission God had given them. Cher, with her medical background, became the resident "physician," as the only other medical help was half a day's journey away. Mike worked with the men of the village and began a labor of love, writing down the unwritten language of the people. Two years later, their first child was born.

As the years went by, Mike and Cher consistently showed God's love and kindness when little was given in return, and slowly the people started to respond, first to their help and friendship and then to the story of God's love for them.

Five difficult, wonderful, demanding, and precious years went by, and the time was approaching for the Riepmas to come back to the states for their first furlough. They looked forward to the reunion with their families, but the thought of leaving their friends, the precious Ese Ejja people, grieved them. They tried to explain that they would be gone for many months but that they would most certainly return.

The people tearfully gathered for a farewell ceremony for the young family they had come to love, and Mike held back the tears when the men of the tribe, who were now his friends and his brothers in Christ, said good-bye. One by one, they removed their shirts and hung them over Mike's shoulders in a show of deep affection.

FRIDAY NIGHT AT MARANATHA was the last time we heard Mike speak. I sat riveted in my chair, listening to the story of what God had done through one couple to reach out to people in great need. Then Mike said something I will never forget.

"Cher and I miss our home in Bolivia and are anxious to get back, but it has been wonderful for us to be here at Maranatha with all of you. There's another reason I'm particularly pleased to be in Michigan this week," he added with a grin, "and that's because I graduated from high school here, and tomorrow night is my ten-year class reunion! I'm really looking forward to seeing some old friends, but I know they'll expect me to pull up in a fancy car, wearing a six-hundred-dollar suit and talking about my impressive job, three homes, and my boat. You see, I was voted the student in my class most likely to succeed. Instead of what they expect, I'm going to show up wearing the one sport coat I own and the suntan I got walking with God in the jungles of Bolivia."

I had tears in my eyes as he closed the meeting in prayer.

They were right, Mike, I thought. Your classmates were right. They may not realize it, but out of their entire class, you were one who truly succeeded in God's eyes. And with your obedience and God's blessing on your life, your dream to serve him successfully in Bolivia is coming true.

I recently spoke with Mike's parents, Paul and Gloria Riepma, and learned that Mike and Cher have now been in Bolivia for twenty-two years. They have four beautiful children, the oldest now in college. And God has greatly blessed their ministry. Cher has trained three Ese Ejja medical helpers, but they are still the only medical resource for many miles. Mike and Cher are both hard at work completing the translation of the Bible into the Ese Ejja language. Life has been difficult but rewarding, and God has been with them every step of the way.

A Whispered Prayer

Dear Heavenly Father, please help me to be faithful to you no matter what my circumstances are. When discouragement comes my way, give me the strength to stay the course and to reflect you with a positive attitude. When faced with temptation, please give me the wisdom and determination to do what is right. Please help me to be a person of integrity. Give me a caring heart for others and an eternal perspective. In the precious name of Jesus, Amen.

Get Up and Go Ideas for Tomorrow

1. As I work and interact with others tomorrow, I will be honest, kind, and patient, and I will smile, remembering that I am representing Jesus to them.
2. If I am being sexually harassed by someone, I will take proper action to protect myself and other potential victims,

and if I am involved in an inappropriate relationship, I will ask God to help me end it.

3. I will ask God for direction in making his dream for my life come true.

A Thought to Ponder as I Fall Asleep

If faced with daily temptation or discouragement, what would I do?

The Scripture Reading: Genesis 39:1–40:5

Now Joseph had been taken down to Egypt. Potiphar, an Egyptian who was one of Pharaoh's officials, the captain of the guard, bought him from the Ishmaelites who had taken him there.

The LORD was with Joseph and he prospered, and he lived in the house of his Egyptian master. When his master saw that the LORD was with him and that the LORD gave him success in everything he did, Joseph found favor in his eyes and became his attendant. Potiphar put him in charge of his household, and he entrusted to his care everything he owned. From the time he put him in charge of his household and of all that he owned, the LORD blessed the household of the Egyptian because of Joseph. The blessing of the LORD was on everything Potiphar had, both in the house and in the field. So he left in Joseph's care everything he had; with Joseph in charge, he did not concern himself with anything except the food he ate.

Now Joseph was well-built and handsome, and after a while his master's wife took notice of Joseph and said, "Come to bed with me!"

But he refused. "With me in charge," he told her, "my master does not concern himself with anything in the house; everything he owns he has entrusted to my care. No one is greater in this house than I am. My master has withheld nothing from me except you, because you are his wife. How then could I do such a wicked thing and sin against God?" And though she spoke to Joseph day after day, he refused to go to bed with her or even be with her.

One day he went into the house to attend to his duties, and none of the household servants was inside. She caught him by his cloak and said, "Come to bed with me!" But he left his cloak in her hand and ran out of the house.

When she saw that he had left his cloak in her hand and had run out of the house, she called her household servants. "Look," she said to them, "this Hebrew has been brought to us to make sport of us! He came in here to sleep with me, but I screamed. When he heard me scream for help, he left his cloak beside me and ran out of the house."

She kept his cloak beside her until his master came home. Then she told him this story: "That Hebrew slave you brought us came to me to make sport of me. But as soon as I screamed for help, he left his cloak beside me and ran out of the house."

When his master heard the story his wife told him, saying, "This is how your slave treated me," he burned with anger. Joseph's master took him and put him in prison, the place where the king's prisoners were confined.

But while Joseph was there in the prison, the LORD was with him; he showed him kindness and granted him favor in the eyes of the prison warden. So the warden put Joseph in charge of all those held in the prison, and he was made responsible for all that was done there. The warden paid no attention to anything under Joseph's care, because the LORD was with Joseph and gave him success in whatever he did.

Some time later, the cupbearer and the baker of the king of Egypt offended their master, the king of Egypt. Pharaoh was angry with his two officials, the chief cupbearer and the chief baker, and put them in custody in the house of the captain of the guard, in the same prison where Joseph was confined. The captain of the guard assigned them to Joseph, and he attended them.

After they had been in custody for some time, each of the two men—the cupbearer and the baker of the king of Egypt, who were being held in prison—had a dream the same night, and each dream had a meaning of its own.

Final Note: The story of Joseph took place approximately 1897–1804 BC. For the complete story of the baker and the cupbearer, Joseph's interpretation of their dreams, and their fulfillment, read Genesis 40:6–23.

FOUR

The Risky Reunion

A Story about Facing the Past and Embracing the Future

Suzanne and John lived with their family in Ontario, Canada. After packing the car and the kids, they headed north for a long-awaited weekend in their humble cabin deep in the woods. Hours later they arrived at their destination, unloaded the vehicle, swept down the cobwebs in the cabin, made up the beds, and crawled in for a good night's rest in the peaceful north country.

Sometime during the night, Suzanne woke in the darkness, feeling a cold shiver across her body. She had no sooner opened her eyes than she felt her husband stiffen beside her. A split second later he was making horrible, tortured sounds and clutching at his chest. Was John having a terrible nightmare or a heart attack? Suzanne didn't know what to do. He was grabbing frantically at his chest and making noises like a crazed animal!

Suddenly, John fell back on his pillow in an exhausted heap. He had broken out in a cold sweat and was lying there shaken and gray-faced. Still clutching his chest, he stared up at the ceiling with haunted eyes.

"Oh, John, darling! Are you all right?" Suzanne grasped his arm in desperation.

He shuddered violently and moistened his lips to speak. "It . . . it . . . it was terrible," he stuttered. "A mm . . . mm . . . mouse . . . got caught inside my . . . pajama top! At first I thought I was dreaming and I couldn't get away from it, but then it was real! It was awful, Suzanne."

John's "dream" turned into reality, but have you ever had a nightmare—the kind of dream that had you tossing and turning or that left you covered in sweat and trembling like a leaf?

There is a story in Scripture about a man who was plagued with a nightmare that left him with a desperate desire to understand what the dream meant. He was Pharaoh, the most powerful man in Egypt.

Joseph's Dreams Come True

With his breaths coming in rapid succession and beads of sweat dotting his forehead, the great Pharaoh moved restlessly in his sleep. Awaking with a start, he struggled to get his bearings; with an exhausted sigh, he realized that he had been dreaming— again. What a night he had endured, with one disturbing dream haunting him on the heels of another!

Shakily he sat up and covered his face with his hands. Never had he been so disturbed by a dream. What could it possibly mean?

As Pharaoh's morning commenced and the uneasy feeling did not leave him, he called for all his wise men and magicians. In great detail he recalled the two dreams for them, but to his dismay and frustration, no one could interpret the meaning.

PHARAOH'S CUPBEARER, who had heard all that was said, remembered two years before, when he had experienced a dream that had left him shaken. With a pang of guilt he realized that, upon being freed, he had promptly forgotten Joseph, the young Hebrew who had interpreted his dream.

Taking a deep breath, he approached his ruler, bowing low before speaking. "Today I am reminded of my shortcomings, great Pharaoh. You may recall that two years ago you were angry with your servants and had two of us imprisoned. While there, we both had strange dreams on the same night, and in the morning we were disturbed over them. A young Hebrew was there with us, and he interpreted our dreams, and things turned out exactly as he said they would. Within three days the baker was hanged, and I was returned to my position of service. The young Hebrew may be able to help you."

JOSEPH'S MORNING BEGAN like every other morning in prison. When he opened his eyes, he wondered fleetingly why God had allowed him to be put in such a place when he had done nothing wrong. Then he resolutely turned his attention to the responsibilities at hand. The fact that he had been made the trustee and put in charge of the other prisoners occupied his mind and body during the day, but it did little to relieve his longing for freedom.

Busy with his duties, he was surprised when royal messengers arrived with the news that he, Joseph, was being summoned to appear before Pharaoh. He gratefully accepted the change of clothing they provided and the opportunity to wash and shave himself. With each swipe of the razor, the oppressive gloom of the dungeon, along with his tangled beard, fell away. His heart thundered as he readied himself. Was he going to be tried for the attempted rape of Potiphar's wife? Had the day of his trial arrived, or did this summons mean something else? His mind clamored for answers, and, in his spirit, he cried out to God.

As Joseph approached the opulent royal chamber, a quiet calm settled over him. Stepping into the large room, he saw the great Pharaoh sitting on a throne, attended by servants. The contrast between this room and the dungeon where he had spent the last several years shocked his senses. Joseph suddenly found himself grateful for the training in courtly manners he had received in Potiphar's household, and he properly presented himself, bowing low before the ruler of Egypt.

PHARAOH STUDIED the handsome young Hebrew as he approached with quiet confidence and impeccable manners. "I have dreamed dreams that no one seems able to interpret," Pharaoh said. "I understand that you have this gift."

"I cannot do it," Joseph replied, "but God will give Pharaoh the answers he desires."

Pharaoh nodded thoughtfully and motioned for Joseph to come closer. "The first dream had seven fat, healthy cows that came up out of the water. Then seven gaunt, sickly cows came up and devoured the healthy ones." Pharaoh closed his eyes for a moment and shook his head at the memory. "I awoke after this disturbing dream but fell asleep again, only to dream of seven healthy heads of grain growing in abundance on one stalk. Then seven other heads sprouted, thin and scorched. Suddenly, the sickly crop swallowed up the seven full heads. I was relieved somewhat to awaken and realize it was a nightmare, but the memory haunts me, and I must know what these strange dreams mean!"

Nodding, Joseph began to speak. "Both dreams have the same meaning, great Pharaoh. God has revealed to you what he is going to do, and it will happen very soon. There will be seven years of great plenty and abundance in this land, but seven desperate years of famine will follow. This famine will be so devastating that the good years will be forgotten."

Suddenly the shadowy horror of those dreams seemed very clear to Pharaoh, and with seriousness he asked, "What can I do to save Egypt from this terrible fate?"

"You need a wise plan and someone to oversee it," Joseph stated quietly. "Find a discerning man and put him in charge of this land. Appoint commissioners to collect one-fifth of the harvest for the first seven years of abundance. Hold the grain in reserve in each city, to be used during the seven years of famine, or without doubt, this country will be devastated."

A hush fell over the room, and Pharaoh instinctively knew that what Joseph had said was true. Taking unprecedented action, Pharaoh then appointed Joseph, the former convict, as the governor of Egypt, second only to Pharaoh himself. He would not only oversee the royal palace, but he would also be in charge of the entire nation. Slipping his own signet ring from his finger, Pharaoh reached for Joseph's hand and placed it on his finger, thereby transferring his authority to the young Hebrew.

WHILE JOSEPH STARED at the ring, trying to take in what was happening, Pharaoh clapped his hands and ordered that rich garments be brought out for Joseph. Soon he was dressed in robes of fine linen. Pharaoh ceremoniously placed a gold chain around his neck. "You will have a fine chariot, and men will go before you, shouting, 'Make way!' Without your permission, no one will lift a hand or a foot."

How his life changed! Pharaoh not only gave Joseph an Egyptian name, Zaphenath-Paneah, but he also decided he should have an Egyptian wife. Her name was Asenath, the daughter of Potiphera, priest of On. How little did Joseph realize at the time of his marriage to the beautiful, high-born stranger that this wife and the children she would bear would bring into his life great joy and healing—a healing he desperately needed after years of emotional pain and misery.

"MAKE WAY! MAKE WAY!" shouted Joseph's attendant, running ahead of the chariot as they entered the last city on Joseph's inspection route. After this last stop, Joseph would head for home and his family. The sun was shining brilliantly, and he took joy in the health and well-being of the people clamoring to get a closer look at him. This was the seventh good year of a bountiful harvest, and not a soul in Egypt lacked food to eat.

Drawing nearer to the immense storage facility, he could see a steady stream of laborers bringing baskets of grain to be weighed and counted. The city commissioner looked up and stepped off the platform to formally greet Joseph, the handsome and powerful governor of all Egypt.

"We are overwhelmed with grain, Your Highness," the commissioner reported, handing him the parchment. "It is like the sands of the sea."

"I have been given the same good report in every area throughout Egypt," Joseph responded. "The total grain in storehouses throughout the land is beyond measure. You have done well, sir, and I entrust the safekeeping of this grain to you, as a time of great need is coming. Pharaoh will be very pleased with your report."

THE DAYS OF PLENTY came to an abrupt end, and famine spread over the entire country and beyond. The ground became parched and dry. The mud flats near the Nile, once fertile and generous, became wrinkled and cracked like the features of a thousand old men. The earth was barren.

The people of Egypt, however, were well-fed and flourishing—because of the wise planning and careful management of Joseph, steward of Pharaoh and servant of the Lord God. As time went on, the vast famine crept beyond the borders of Egypt to cover the ancient world. Many journeyed to Egypt hoping to buy grain.

The storehouses had been opened in each city, and the commissioners were assigned to sell the grain at a fair price to the people, being careful to ration the grain so it would meet the needs of the nation for the full seven years the famine would last. Day after day, Joseph himself met with Egyptians and foreigners alike who petitioned for food in the capital city.

Looking up one afternoon from the effusive thanks of a man who had been granted a grain purchase, Joseph was startled to see a group of dusty, bearded men being directed toward him. He found himself involuntarily counting how many were in the group, and the shock that ran through him as he recognized his ten older brothers almost unseated him.

As the men bowed with their faces to the ground, the oldest spoke for all of them. "Oh, great Zaphenath-Paneah, governor of all Egypt, we are your humble servants who have come to buy grain for our starving families."

He doesn't recognize me, Joseph thought. The realization amazed him until he silently acknowledged that he not only looked different than he had twenty-two years ago but also that none of his brothers had ever expected to see him again.

They've aged, Joseph thought, noting graying beards and receding hairlines. Then with slight amusement, *And they're afraid of me.* Feigning boredom, he turned to his interpreter, requesting him to translate.

"Who are you and where do you come from?" he asked harshly and motioned for the interpreter to relate his question to them.

"We are ten brothers, the sons of one man from the land of Canaan, here to buy grain," Reuben offered nervously. "We have one other brother at home, and one is deceased."

The others continued prostrate on the ground, and Joseph suddenly recalled his youthful dream, in which one day they would all bow before him. This brought him little joy as his emotions churned with painful memories of the past.

"You are spies here to see where our land is vulnerable!" Turning to his guards, he gave the order for them to be taken into custody.

HE LET THEM SWEAT IT OUT in the very dungeon where he had spent years of his life, while his own mind was teeming with questions. Was his father well? Had they mistreated his younger brother, Benjamin, like they had mistreated him? Had they changed? Overriding all these questions was a strange longing to help these, his own people. But could he trust them?

Perhaps he could test them without revealing his identity, and see with his own eyes that Benjamin was all right.

Three days later, ten bedraggled, sober, and frightened brothers stood before him.

"You say you are brothers. Is your father still living?" Relieved when they affirmed that their elderly father was still alive, Joseph continued. "You claim to be honest men. Well, here is your test." He motioned for his interpreter to relay his message. "Do this, and you will live, for I fear God. One of you will stay here in prison while the rest of you go and take back grain for your starving households. But you must bring your youngest brother to me, so that your words may be proved and so that you will not die!"

Hearing the news, they turned to one another in anguish, speaking in Hebrew among themselves. "Surely this is our punishment for what we did to our brother Joseph! We saw how distressed he was when we mistreated him, and how he pleaded for his life, but we would not listen!"

Then Reuben, the oldest, spoke up in irritation. "You wouldn't listen to me when I told you not to sin against the boy! Now we may have to give an accounting for his blood!"

Joseph listened, taking in every harsh word and quarrelsome tone. The vivid reminder of his terror on that awful day made the memory as raw and painful as an open wound. Anger and grief overwhelmed him for a moment, and tears stung his eyes. Joseph turned away from them until he gained control of his emotions and then turned back, harshly barking an order to his guards. Simeon was bound before their eyes and taken from them.

UPON RETURNING to the land of Canaan, nine sober brothers had disturbing news for their father, Jacob. Yes, they had returned with grain, but the governor of Egypt had treated them harshly and accused them of being spies. He had imprisoned them, and, upon their release, had held back Simeon, who would not be released until they returned with their youngest brother, Benjamin, to prove that they were telling the truth.

"There is more disturbing news, Father," Judah said, producing a heavy sack of grain and untying the rope at the top. "We brought back grain, but we have all examined our sacks, and the money, which each of us paid for our grain, has been found in the mouth of each sack. No one apprehended us upon leaving, but could this be a trick to prove us thieves?"

Taking the pouch from his son and turning it over in his gnarled hands, Jacob felt fear sweep through him. Then Reuben, the eldest, spoke up. "Put Benjamin in my trust, Father, and if I do not bring him back safely, you can put both of my own sons to death."

"No!" Jacob said. "I have lost Joseph, and now Simeon! I refuse to send Benjamin with you. If something were to happen to him, grief would send me to my grave."

TIME PASSED, and still famine crippled the earth. The grain was gone, and other supplies were low. Calling his sons together, Jacob instructed them to go back to Egypt once again.

"We cannot do that, Father," Reuben said for them all. "The Egyptian warned us that we would not see Simeon's face again until we had Benjamin with us."

"Why did you bring trouble upon us by even telling him you had another brother?" Jacob asked in exasperation.

Judah spoke up. "He questioned us closely about ourselves and our family, Father. How could we have known he would order us to bring our brother to him? Send the boy along with me, and we will leave at once, so that we and our families will live."

Kneeling before Jacob, Judah swore an oath to his father. "I myself guarantee Benjamin's safety; you can hold me personally responsible for him. If I fail to bring him back, I will bear the blame before you all my life. As it is, Father, we could have gone and returned twice by now!"

With a weary sigh, Jacob relented, instructing them to bring gifts of honey and spices, pistachio nuts and almonds, to the governor of Egypt. He also had them take double the amount of silver to pay not only for what they would buy but also for the grain the family had already eaten.

"WHAT DO YOU THINK he intends to do? If we do not bring Benjamin back with us, our father will die!" the brothers whispered to one another as they were ushered into the governor's own home for the second time in two days. The bizarre events that had occurred since they had arrived in the capital city terrified them.

First, they had been sent to the governor's home, where they were reunited with Simeon and served a meal. To their surprise, the ruler then seated them at the table in order of their age, from oldest to youngest. The governor had seemed to like Benjamin very much and had shown him favor. But then, upon leaving the next morning, each with his load of grain, they were apprehended by Joseph's steward, who demanded the return of his master's silver cup. The brothers swore none of them had taken it, but when the steward searched them, not only did he find a double portion of silver in each of their sacks but also the silver cup in Benjamin's sack. The boy was terrified, and his brothers were beside themselves with fear and consternation.

Joseph was waiting for them as they came back and threw themselves at his feet. "What is this you have done?" he asked.

"What can we say, my lord? How can we prove our innocence? We are all your slaves!"

"Nonsense," Joseph said, watching his brothers carefully as his words were translated to them. "Only the man who was found to have my cup will pay for this transgression. The rest of you may go back to your aged father."

At that, Judah stepped forward and reached a trembling hand out toward Joseph. "Please allow me, your servant, to speak. The boy is the only child left of his mother, as his brother is no more, and our father dearly loves him. If he is not with us when we return, our father will die. I, your servant, guaranteed the boy's safety to my father and said that I would bear the blame before him all of my life. Please let me remain here as my lord's slave in place of the boy and let him return with my brothers!" Judah's voice broke with emotion. "How can I go back to my father without the boy? No! Do not let me see the misery that would come upon my father."

JOSEPH COULD BARELY contain himself. *They really have changed*, he realized. *They truly honor our father and seek to protect, rather than to harm, Benjamin. And Judah—what a turnabout from the man who proposed selling me as a slave!*

"Have everyone leave my presence!" he cried out in Egyptian to his attendants. They scurried to obey, and for the first time, Joseph was left alone with his brothers. He lost the battle to control his emotions, and he wept aloud, which frightened his brothers even more and alarmed the Egyptians in his household who could hear him.

Wiping his eyes with the back of his hand, he spoke to his brothers in Hebrew for the first time. "I am Joseph! Is my father truly still living?"

Struck dumb with fear, his brothers could not answer him.

Tears were running down Joseph's face. "It is true! Come close to me," he urged them, motioning for them to gather around. "I am your brother Joseph, the one you sold into Egypt many years ago!"

At their astonishment and fear, he rushed to reassure them. "Do not be afraid, and do not be angry with yourselves for selling me, because it was to save lives that God sent me ahead of you. For two years there has been a great famine in the land, and it will go on for another five years. God has told me this, and now

I realize that he has sent me ahead of you to deliver you and all our family."

Shock and fear turned into astonishment as they took in the words of the brother they had betrayed so long ago. Several dropped to their knees. Tears of shame and regret dampened their beards, and they looked at one another and back at Joseph, shaking their heads in wonder.

"It was not you who sent me here, but God," Joseph reassured them again, "and he has made me lord of all Egypt. I want you to hurry home to our father and give him this message: 'Come to Egypt and don't delay. Bring your children and grandchildren, your flocks and herds, and all you have. I will provide for you in the region of Goshen, and you will be near me.'"

Throwing his arms around Benjamin, he wept over the young man who reminded him so much of himself early in life. From brother to brother, Joseph reached out to embrace them and wept over them. After that, they sat and talked, answering his questions about the family he had missed and discussing the move that would take the children of Israel to a new land.

Digging Deeper

Have time for a little trivia? Egyptian men always shaved. Only the pharaoh wore a beard, and that was fake—usually wooden.[1] When Joseph cleaned up for his appointment with Pharaoh, the Scripture says he shaved. Joseph's Hebrew brothers, on the other hand, wore beards. As governor, with his Egyptian haircut, headdress, shaved face, and attire, Joseph was not recognized by his brothers, but he most certainly recognized them.

How old was Joseph when he finally realized his dreams had come true? We know that Joseph was 17 years old when his brothers sold him into slavery. I was curious about the time line for the other outstanding events of his life and found some fascinating information in *Fausset's Bible Dictionary*, which told me that when Joseph was 17 and sold by his brothers, his father, Jacob, was 108 years old, and that his grandfather, Isaac, was still living! (Isaac died 12 years later.)

Joseph was 30 years old when he was made governor, which means that he completed his teens and grew into manhood while in Potiphar's household. He was probably in his mid-twenties when he was victimized by Potiphar's wife and subsequently thrown into prison. We know that the king's cupbearer waited 2 years after being restored to Pharaoh's court to "remember" that Joseph had interpreted his dream, so we can figure that Joseph spent the rest of his twenties polishing his leadership and organizational skills in prison. Governor of Egypt at age 30, Joseph was 39 years old when he was reunited with his father.[2] By that time he had fathered 2 sons himself. What a life! (By the way, Joseph lived to be 110 years old, long enough to hold his grandchildren and great-grandchildren on his knees.)

Why did Joseph test his brothers so rigorously? Let's face it. They had to jump through some pretty big hoops to get the grain they had come for. Accusing them of being spies, Joseph imprisoned them for three days. I have to admit that the news brought me some personal satisfaction! Putting some deeper thought into it, however, I believe it was important for the brothers to experience just a taste of the fear and painful uncertainty that Joseph had lived with for years, because later, when they learned the truth of what had happened to him, they would better understand the cost Joseph had paid for their own sinful actions.

Seeing them again brought Joseph great joy and great anguish. Had they changed? He had to know! They left after their first visit, leaving Simeon behind. Did Joseph figure this would guarantee their return? It's interesting to note that once they reported their Egyptian adventure to their father, little mention is made of Simeon, who was left in rather desperate straits, incarcerated in an Egyptian dungeon. (However long he was there did not compare with Joseph's prison experience.) What finally brought his brothers back was that they were desperate to get more grain to feed their families.

Why did Joseph pick Simeon to stay imprisoned in Egypt? We're not told here, but I wonder if he remembered Simeon treating him more violently than some of the others. Simeon had a history of violence, which is recorded in Genesis 34.

Joseph desperately wanted his father and their entire family to come and stay in the safe haven he could provide, but before that could happen, he exercised some tough love. Each test was further proof that his brothers had changed. When he finally saw Benjamin, and when he heard Judah's impassioned and selfless offer to enslave himself rather than leave Benjamin behind and grieve their father, he was convinced. (To read the entire story of the tests Joseph gave his brothers before revealing himself to them, and about his reunion with his father, read Genesis 42–44.)

Why did Joseph cry at their reunion? In spite of his hard life, Joseph was clearly a sensitive man, and several times in this story we see him deeply moved by emotion. In fact, in this story, Joseph weeps more than any other biblical character.[3] Weeping over past pain is certainly understandable; however, in the reunion scene, we see something a little different. Here Joseph offers unconditional love and forgiveness to some undeserving rascals. Although, at the same time, he is so overwhelmed with the realization that God's great hand had been at work in all their lives that he literally weeps aloud for joy! Finally free of the feelings of hatred and betrayal, he says, "Come close to me . . . do not be distressed and do not be angry with yourselves for selling me here, because it was to save lives that God sent me ahead of you . . . to save your lives by a great deliverance" (Gen. 45:4–7). He was free from his depression over the past, was ready to love and even comfort those who had wronged him, and would trust God with the future.

How can this story apply to your life?

My friend Marilyn Cripps has lived a remarkable life of selfless service to the Lord. She worked in service industries as a tailor and caterer for many years, using her free time to cater church dinners and to open her home to missionaries, youth groups, and anyone else who needed encouragement. Soon after retirement, Marilyn lost her sight and is now legally blind. But she still shares her gifts by teaching a Bible study in the women's county jail every other week, and she has a powerful personal prayer ministry. Rather than being bitter over losing her sight, she has an amazingly positive attitude. Right now I can hear her voice saying, "The best thing about growing older is looking back and seeing how very faithful God has been."

I can imagine Joseph saying those exact words when he reached the end of his life. "The best thing about growing older is looking back and seeing how very faithful God has been."

How is your outlook on life, past, present, and future? Ask yourself a few questions:

- When I reflect on my life, can I see that there were times when God was able to use a difficult circumstance (or even something someone else meant to harm me) for good in my life instead?
- Is reconciliation needed in my family, my church, or my workplace?
- Could God use me as a catalyst to bring about a reunion in which we all hug and laugh and cry together?

Joseph represents a type of Christ, exhibiting unconditional love where it is not deserved—in his case, not only forgiving his brothers but also providing for their salvation with life-giving food and a home with him. Jesus did the same and far better for us when he loved us unconditionally, paid the price for our sin on the cross of Calvary, and provided a home with him in heaven for all who choose to accept his gift of salvation.

In Ephesians 2:13–14, Paul describes how Jesus Christ destroys barriers. "You who once were far away have been brought near through the blood of Christ. For he himself is our peace, who has made the two one and has destroyed the barrier, the dividing wall of hostility."

I CLOSE THIS CHAPTER about Joseph's reunion with his brothers by sharing another story about a reunion that occurred in my life some years ago.

When I first started my speaking ministry, I felt so honored to receive invitations that I mistakenly felt I should say yes to every opportunity. As a result, I became overbooked and sometimes felt overwhelmed.

Looking ahead on my schedule one evening, I realized that the week ahead would include three speaking engagements with one overnight. I felt exhausted before the week even began.

Turning to my husband, I asked, "Honey, if Amber Joy and I are still asleep when you wake up on Friday morning, would you mind if we just slept in? I need a little more sleep before the weekend actually begins."

Friday morning came, and my husband, Graydon, got up, tiptoed around, unplugged the telephone so we would not be disturbed, kissed me on the nose, and left for work. I slumbered on. When I finally woke up, it was 9:15 a.m., and our three-year-old daughter was still asleep. Crawling out of bed, I dragged myself to the closet and surveyed the contents. I hadn't chosen my outfit the night before, so in a sleepy stupor, I stared at the array of garments, dumbly waiting for just the right outfit to leap out at me.

My mind lifted out of the fog for a moment as I considered my options. *Do I want to take my shower now, shave my legs, wash and do my hair, and get all ready for that conference I have to leave for later today?* Noting the time on the bedside clock, I quickly rejected that idea. I had at least five hours that were all mine.

I didn't do any of the aforementioned tasks and instead pulled on a stained sweatshirt of my husband's. Next, I stepped into a pair of old blue jeans—not nice, form-fitting, tummy-tucking jeans, mind you—these were comfy, baggy jeans with an elastic waistband and legs that were so short my ankles hung out the bottoms. (This was long before capri pants were in fashion.) Picture this hideous fashion plate without a spot of makeup on her face and with hair untouched by a hairbrush, let alone shampoo, and my portrait would be about complete.

Amber woke up and looked almost as bad as I did. She was wearing a hand-me-down blanket sleeper from one of her cousins. It had a big hole in the left knee, and her toes stuck out of the flopping left foot. Her hair was a ratty halo around her head, and she had big sleep goobers in the corners of her eyes.

We were a sight, but our morning together was wonderful. During breakfast, I marveled at how quiet the house was. The phone hadn't even rung! Then we headed for the big enclosed front porch. It was our favorite room, with a big wicker rocker, fireplace, and sunshine pouring in. We rocked together in the rocker, talking and giggling. Then I reached for the television remote control and clicked on *The Richard Simmons Show*.

I'd never been very athletic, rarely one to attempt an exercise regimen, but the program, which happened to be for seniors that day, caught my attention. The music was catchy, and I turned to Amber and said, "Hey, honey, let's exercise with the grandmas on the program!" It sounded fun to her, so we got into position. I happened to be standing with my back to the front door (which had nine window panes in it). The music started, and we clumsily threw ourselves into the leg lifts demonstrated on screen, giggling together when Amber's foot jutted farther and farther out of her pajamas.

Unexpectedly, a loud knock sounded on the door directly behind me. I froze with my foot in midair and then swiveled around to see who had caught me. *Oh no!* I felt like I was dying a rapid death. Standing on the step with his nose pressed to the glass and a grin on his face was Mike Hollenbeck, an old boyfriend from high school I hadn't seen in years!

It was too late to run; he had already seen me. With my heart in my big toe, I turned and walked the two remaining steps to the front door. Covering my face with my left hand and peering between my fingers, I opened the door with my right hand.

"Mike! How wonderful to see you!" I blurted. Without removing my left hand from my face, I gestured toward Amber with my right. "Mike, this is my daughter, Amber. Amber, this is Mike."

He was chuckling! I was mortified. "Ah, Mike, why don't you just take a seat here on the front porch and visit with Amber for a few minutes . . . while I go comb my hair!"

I hastily backed out of the room and raced for the bathroom, where I frantically applied a little makeup. (I didn't want to put too much on, for fear the change would be too drastic!) As I dragged a comb through my hair, I thought fleetingly of several old boyfriends I had bumped into over the years, and how I had always thought with great relief, *Am I ever glad I didn't end up with him!* I had the sick feeling Mike was out on the front porch, thinking that about me!

Taking a deep breath, I headed for the porch. What awaited me was a wonderful visit with an old friend. I found out that God had gotten ahold of Mike's life. He and his wife, Joyce, were working for a large Christian camp in central Michigan, and he was planning to enter seminary in the fall. Traveling across the state on camp business that day, Mike had driven through our small town of Fremont. Stopping at a light, he noticed a building with a sign that said GRAYDON W. DIMKOFF, ATTORNEY AND COUNSELOR AT LAW and thought to himself, *Isn't that the guy Jennie Afman married?* He pulled into a parking place, entered the building, met Graydon, and asked where we lived so he could stop by and see me.

With a chuckle he added, "You probably don't know that your husband tried to give you a call to warn you I was coming." His grin got bigger. "I believe your phone is unplugged."

No wonder the house had been so quiet! I tried to laugh it off, all the while thinking, *If I would have had some warning about this little reunion, I would have gone all out to make myself look good—if only to show you what you missed!*

But, alas, no such warning came, and what Mike found was . . . reality.

As the days went by following that visit, I found myself blushing at the mere thought of my circumstances that day. If only I had known he was stopping by! Then one day, another thought struck me. *One of these days, I'm going to be running around at my everyday hectic pace, and unexpectedly there'll be a knock at the door. Who will be standing there to meet me? God—because my life will have ended.*

Do you realize that every single one of us will one day answer the same door? The question is, how will I respond? Will I have to cover my face in shame and embarrassment at how God found me? Will I be stammering out excuses such as "Oh, God! It's wonderful to see you, but I wasn't really expecting this visit today. Ah, could you wait over here a little while so I can quickly get my life in order? Could you just wait while I get something straight with my husband or tell my daughter that you love her? I really meant to do that."

Too late, eternity's begun.

And what would be the saddest thing of all? If I opened the door and recognized God for who he is, but he didn't recognize me as his child—because I had never made a conscious choice to invite him to be my heavenly Father. God's Word explains that he does not come into our lives uninvited (Rev. 3:20), but that he stands at the door of our lives and knocks, waiting to be asked in.

Have you invited him into your life? Bottom line, do you have a personal relationship with God? Do you need one?

I simply cannot close this chapter without encouraging you to make that life-changing decision. If you need a relationship with God and want to invite him into your life, please open your heart to him today. Tell God that you need to know him and that you accept the gift of salvation offered by the sacrifice of his Son, Jesus. The simple prayer given below can help you to do this.

A Whispered Prayer

Dear God, I need you in my life! I admit that I am a sinner. I have done wrong things, but I do believe that you love me and that you sent your son, Jesus, to pay for my sin on the cross of Calvary. Please forgive my past and make me brand new. Thank you for the miracle you have begun in my heart today. Help me to grow to know you better. Thank you for the reunion that awaits us when we meet one day, face to face. In the precious name of Jesus, Amen.

Get Up and Go Ideas for Tomorrow

1. I will spend time in the Bible, God's Word, and in prayer, so that I will get to know him better.
2. I will ask God to give me a heart of forgiveness toward those who have hurt me in the past and to bring healing and joy into my life.

A Thought to Ponder as I Fall Asleep

Would I be embarrassed or ashamed if God literally came to my door and saw my life as I lived it today?

The Scripture Reading: Genesis 41:14–16, 25–49, 53–54, 56–57; 42:1–2, 5; 45:1–10, 13–14

So Pharaoh sent for Joseph, and he was quickly brought from the dungeon. When he had shaved and changed his clothes, he came before Pharaoh.

Pharaoh said to Joseph, "I had a dream, and no one can interpret it. But I have heard it said of you that when you hear a dream you can interpret it."

"I cannot do it," Joseph replied to Pharaoh, "but God will give Pharaoh the answer he desires. . . ."

Then Joseph said to Pharaoh, "The dreams of Pharaoh are one and the same. God has revealed to Pharaoh what he is about to do. The seven good cows are seven years, and the seven good heads of grain are seven years; it is one and the same dream. The seven lean, ugly cows that came up afterward are seven years, and so are the seven worthless heads of grain scorched by the east wind: They are seven years of famine. . . .

"God has shown Pharaoh what he is about to do. Seven years of great abundance are coming throughout the land of Egypt, but seven years of famine will follow them. Then all the abundance in Egypt will be forgotten, and the famine will ravage the land. The abundance in the land will not be remembered, because the famine that follows it will be so severe. The reason the dream was given to Pharaoh in two forms is that the matter has been firmly decided by God, and God will do it soon.

"And now let Pharaoh look for a discerning and wise man and put him in charge of the land of Egypt. Let Pharaoh appoint commissioners over the land to take a fifth of the harvest of Egypt during the seven years of abundance. They should collect all the food of these good years that are coming and store up the grain under the authority of Pharaoh, to be kept in the cities for food. This food should be held in reserve for the country, to be used during the seven years of famine that will come upon Egypt, so that the country may not be ruined by the famine."

The plan seemed good to Pharaoh and to all his officials. So Pharaoh asked them, "Can we find anyone like this man, one in whom is the spirit of God?"

Then Pharaoh said to Joseph, "Since God has made all this known to you, there is no one so discerning and wise as you. You shall be in charge of my palace, and all my people are to submit to your orders. Only with respect to the throne will I be greater than you."

So Pharaoh said to Joseph, "I hereby put you in charge of the whole land of Egypt." Then Pharaoh took his signet ring from his finger and put it on Joseph's finger. He dressed him in robes of fine linen and put a gold chain around his neck. He had him ride in a chariot as his second-in-command, and men shouted before him, "Make way!" Thus he put him in charge of the whole land of Egypt.

Then Pharaoh said to Joseph, "I am Pharaoh, but without your word no one will lift hand or foot in all Egypt." Pharaoh gave Joseph the name Zaphenath-Paneah and gave him Asenath daughter of Potiphera, priest of On, to be his wife. . . .

Joseph was thirty years old when he entered the service of Pharaoh king of Egypt. And Joseph went out from Pharaoh's presence and traveled throughout Egypt. During the seven years of abundance the land produced plentifully. Joseph collected all the food produced in those seven years of abundance in Egypt and stored it in the cities. In each city he put the food grown in the fields surrounding it. Joseph stored up huge quantities of grain, like the sand of the sea; it was so much that he stopped keeping records because it was beyond measure....

The seven years of abundance in Egypt came to an end, and the seven years of famine began, just as Joseph had said. There was famine in all the other lands, but in the whole land of Egypt there was food....

When the famine had spread over the whole country, Joseph opened the storehouses and sold grain to the Egyptians, for the famine was severe throughout Egypt. And all the countries came to Egypt to buy grain from Joseph, because the famine was severe in all the world.

When Jacob learned that there was grain in Egypt, he said to his sons, "Why do you just keep looking at each other?" He continued, "I have heard that there is grain in Egypt. Go down there and buy some for us, so that we may live and not die." ...

So Israel's sons were among those who went to buy grain, for the famine was in the land of Canaan also....

Then Joseph could no longer control himself before all his attendants, and he cried out, "Have everyone leave my presence!" So there was no one with Joseph when he made himself known to his brothers. And he wept so loudly that the Egyptians heard him, and Pharaoh's household heard about it.

Joseph said to his brothers, "I am Joseph! Is my father still living?" But his brothers were not able to answer him, because they were terrified at his presence.

Then Joseph said to his brothers, "Come close to me." When they had done so, he said, "I am your brother Joseph, the one you sold into Egypt! And now, do not be distressed and do not be angry with yourselves for selling me here, because it was to save lives that God sent me ahead of you. For two years now there has been famine in the land, and for the next five years there will not be plowing and reaping. But God sent me ahead of you to preserve for you a remnant on earth and to save your lives by a great deliverance.

"So then, it was not you who sent me here, but God.... Now hurry back to my father and say to him, 'This is what your son Joseph says: God has made me lord of all Egypt. Come down to me; don't delay. You shall live in the region of Goshen and be near me....'

"Tell my father about all the honor accorded me in Egypt and about everything you have seen. And bring my father down here quickly."

Then he threw his arms around his brother Benjamin and wept....

Final Note: Joseph's entire life story is found in Genesis 37–50 and was recorded by Moses some time between 1450–1410 BC.[4] Joseph is also mentioned in the New Testament in Hebrews 11:22. He and his eleven brothers and their families multiplied in the land of Egypt and became known as the twelve tribes of Israel.

Lost and Found

A Story about the Power of God's Word

Standing at the door of her inner-city classroom, Miss Amber Dimkoff greeted each third grader with a warm smile, a handshake, and a personal greeting. "Good morning, Daysha. Good morning, Earl. Good morning, Danielle. My, your braids look pretty this morning! Good morning, Janiqua. Did you bring back the paper I sent home with you yesterday? Please place it on my desk. Good morning, Tajh." She went through the same routine at the start of each school day. "Good morning, Jamison. Good morning, Jamal." The list went on.

When the last straggler had made it through the door, Miss Dimkoff instructed the students to put away their backpacks and take their seats. Surveying her charges, who included the traditional eight-year-olds and an assortment of older students who had been held back for various reasons, she noticed little Jamal sitting with his elbows on his desk, his chin in his hands and a bleak expression on his small face.

"Are you all right this morning, Jamal?" Miss Dimkoff asked.

"I'm kinda sad today," he said.

"Would you like to talk about it?"

"No," he responded, shaking his head.

"Would you like to write me a note?" Miss Dimkoff suggested with an encouraging smile.

"Okay" was his simple response. He tugged a piece of paper out of his notebook, wrote one line, and handed the paper to his teacher. *My brother died yesterday.*

After folding the note and praying for wisdom, Miss Dimkoff tucked the paper in her pocket. Stooping down beside his desk she said quietly, "Would you like to have lunch with me today?"

His eyes met hers solemnly, and he nodded.

That night a weary young teacher phoned her mom in Michigan. My daughter's voice sounded even more tired than usual. "Mom, Jamal's brother Jerome was murdered last night! Jamal said he didn't know who shot him, but that Jerome's girlfriend and his two little boys were sad today too. The boy who died had two children of his own." Amber sighed.

"Jamal was obviously thinking a lot about death today, so I talked about heaven and said that if we know and love God, we can look forward to going there when we die, which seemed to comfort him. Can you believe he was sent to school today?" Frustrated, she went on. "Oh Mom, sometimes this job seems hopeless! So many of these kids come from violent or abusive backgrounds. I have one little boy whose father tried to strangle

114

him a few months ago. I have three kids with severe anger management problems, and there is only one child in my classroom who lives with both of his parents. It seems like the cycle of poverty and neglect is never ending, and I see it reflected in these kids every day." She heaved a huge sigh. "When I came to Baltimore to teach, I really believed I could make a difference, but I'm so tired and discouraged. Please pray for me, and for the kids in my class. Their lives seem to be caught in such a downward spiral."

"I'm sure that's true in some cases, honey," I responded. "But Amber, *never* feel that you can't make a difference. Ask God to help you to model godly leadership in front of your third graders and to help you to raise up another leader. You can't change the past for these kids, but with God's help, honey, you can impact the life and future of one, or maybe two or more, and they in turn will affect the lives of many others."

IT MAY SEEM like people always reflect the environment in which they were raised, but if that's true, the future looks mighty bleak for countless people in the world today. What we need to remember is that no matter where we come from, we have the freedom to make choices that will affect ourselves and others —most importantly, the choice to know and love God and to allow him to direct our lives.

If we fast-forward in history from Joseph's story (approximately 1800 BC) to approximately 700–500 BC, we find a record in Scripture about the reigns of the kings of Israel, and specifically the kingdoms of Judah. I'm sad to say that some of these kings were evil rulers who, in turn, created an evil environment for their families and their people. One such king was Manasseh, the son of Hezekiah, who is credited with being one of the most wicked of Judah's kings. He defiled the temple of God with heathen altars

115

and idols, practiced the occult, and sacrificed his own sons as burnt offerings to the pagan god Molech, and tradition holds that he killed Isaiah the prophet by having him sawed in two.[1] His own son, Amon, was a product of that environment and followed in all his father's evil ways.

But what we should note is that Amon's son, Josiah, who was left fatherless at age eight, rejected the examples of his father and grandfather and changed the course of history during his lifetime. He refused to be a product of his past, and instead harkened after his ancestor King David. He is an example in courage, commitment, and leadership for us all.

Josiah's Story

Uncertain as to what had awakened him, the small eight-year-old boy stiffened and stared into the darkness, trying to make sense of the muffled sounds coming from outside his bedchamber. Low voices issued curt orders, and the boy heard the sound of hurrying footsteps. He recognized one angry voice in the distance when his father cursed. There was the sound of a short scuffle. Then the sound of footsteps scurried away and all was quiet.

What's going on? the boy wondered with a slight shiver. Just then, his mother, Jedidah, slipped quietly into the room.

"Josiah," she whispered urgently. "Are you awake?"

Sitting up, he reached out and was enclosed in her warm arms.

"My precious son," she whispered, hugging him briefly, "we must hurry and hide, for evil abounds in this place tonight."

Together they slipped through the small door that led to her quarters and then out into a servant's hall, where they were met by his mother's guard.

"What has happened, Mother, and why must we hide?" Josiah asked her an hour later when they were settled in the home of trusted servants.

Cupping her son's small face, Jedidah studied him for a moment. "Your father was assassinated tonight, Josiah. Do you understand? He has been killed. His own servants plotted against him, and I have to make sure you're safe until we know what will be done."

My father is dead? Josiah's mind reeled with the news. He'd never been close to his father, and recently had feared him. Steeped in occult worship and witchcraft, Amon had followed in his own father's footsteps, allowing infant sacrifices to the pagan god Molech. The horror of those sacrifices and the memory of his mother weeping would forever be etched in grief on Josiah's young heart.

The news spread quickly, and within days the people of Jerusalem rose up and executed all who had conspired against King Amon. Jedidah and her young son were escorted back to the palace, where eight-year-old Josiah was crowned the king of Judah.

Born when his father was only sixteen years old, Josiah had known since earliest childhood that he was the heir to the throne of Judah. However, since Josiah's grandfather had reigned for fifty-five years and his father had become king only two years before, the throne had been only a distant thought to the little boy.

Standing next to a pillar on a high platform, with his father's royal robe hanging from his small shoulders and the weight of the golden crown slipping over one ear, King Josiah listened to the cheering crowds. Glancing to his left, he caught his mother's reassuring smile and remembered her whispered encouragement that morning. "Don't be afraid, Josiah, God will be with you."

THE NEXT EIGHT YEARS saw Josiah growing into his father's robe, but at no time did he follow in his father's habits or lifestyle. During those formative years he was educated in language, mathematics, religion, and government. Josiah lived in Jerusalem, and life for the people in the kingdom around him went on in much the same way it had when his father and grandfather ruled. However, in childlike faith, Josiah did what was right in the sight of the Lord God and did not waver from it, hearkening after his famous forefather King David.

When Josiah was sixteen, in the eighth year of his reign, his faith took an even deeper turn. He hungered after an intimate relationship with God. On his own he sought after God, and for the next four years he dedicated himself to that pursuit.

SUMMONING HIS SECRETARY, the young king announced what had been on his mind and heart for some time. "Shaphan, please call for the high priest and my other advisors. I have decided to institute some rather radical changes in the land, and I would like them to understand my thinking."

Shaphan hurried to do Josiah's bidding. He had watched his young king grow into manhood, and now, at age twenty, Josiah was emerging as a leader with personal discipline and deep commitment. It was a pleasure to serve such a monarch.

And so, under the clear direction of King Josiah, in the twelfth year of his reign, reformation began in Jerusalem and throughout Judah. The assignment was immense, as the worship of pagan deities was rampant. But nevertheless, Josiah had carved idols destroyed and cast images crushed to powder. The altars to Baal were torn down, and the incense altars that were above them were literally cut to pieces.

Josiah found particular relief in destroying Topheth, which was also known as "the Fireplace." It was on that pagan altar, located just outside Jerusalem, that parents sacrificed their own children. Bile rose in Josiah's throat as he recalled vivid memories of the sound of drumbeats and the smell of burning flesh as children were sacrificed to the god Molech in a grotesque commitment to idolatry.

Josiah desecrated the high places, insuring they would not be used again. The pagan priests who had offered sacrifices were themselves put to death, their bones burned on their own altars. Leaving Israel, Josiah went on to the towns of Simeon, Manasseh, Ephram, Naphtali, and beyond, purging the land of evil, sorcery, and idolatry. While there, he collected money from the people for the repair of the temple in Jerusalem. The six-year campaign was long and exhausting, but the young ruler was single-minded in his resolve. There had never before been a king like him.

WHEN HE RETURNED to Jerusalem, Josiah focused his attention on the restoration of the temple. It was the eighteenth year of his reign, and he was twenty-six years old.

Calling together Shaphan, his trusted secretary, Maaseidah, the ruler of the city, and Joah, the recorder, he instructed them regarding the repairs and told them to go to Hilkiah, the high priest.

"I want you to take the funds that were collected during the campaign, and also the money that the Levites have collected, and meet with Hilkiah, who in turn should choose faithful supervisors to entrust it to. These men will oversee the work on the Lord's temple."

Josiah's instructions were carried out, and Hilkiah, the high priest, appointed honest men who in turn paid the carpenters, masons, and artisans, and who also purchased timber for joists and beams to repair the temple buildings that the kings of Judah had allowed to fall into ruin.

As Shaphan walked through the temple gates, his eyes surveyed the construction project going on before him, and a sense of fulfillment overwhelmed him for a moment. So much had been accomplished in the six years since Josiah had started his reforms. At times it amazed him that one so young could have made such a difference. With a sigh of satisfaction, he went on to his appointment with Hilkiah. He would then bring back a progress report to his king.

Hilkiah met him upon his arrival and ushered him inside. "The work is indeed going well, and the workers are men of integrity who are accomplishing their assignments in a timely and trustworthy fashion." Then, turning aside to a table behind him, the priest lifted a dusty scroll and handed it to the king's secretary. "In the renovation process, a book has been discovered in the temple of the Lord. It is the Book of the Law."

Shaphan returned to King Josiah with the book in hand. First giving Josiah the temple restoration report, he then informed the king about the book. "Hilkiah the priest has given me a book that was found in the ruin of the temple. It is the Book of the Law. Would you like me to read it to you?"

"What? You say you have found the word of the Lord? How could something so priceless have been mislaid?" Stunned by the unexpected discovery, Josiah sat back on his throne and nodded for Shaphan to begin. He was well aware that the discovery was a treasure beyond value, and the young king who had sought after God with his whole heart listened with every fiber of his being.

What Josiah heard that day left him grieved to his very core. Shaphan read the laws for living and worship that were pleasing to God and the instructions for celebrating the great Passover, which had been neglected by the Israelites for generations.

He read of the Lord God's anger over the disobedience of his people. As Josiah listened, sorrow over the sin of his father, his grandfather, and his people engulfed him.

The young king of Judah wept aloud and tore his robes, realizing that the sin of the nation was great and the wrath of God was imminent.

SHAPHAN, HILKIAH, AHIKAM (who was Shaphan's grown son), Achbor, and Asaian, the king's servant, assembled before Josiah a short time later and received their instructions.

"I want you to go and inquire of the Lord for me and for the remnant of Israelites about what is written in this book that has been found," he said in great earnest. "I fear that the Lord's anger will be poured out on us because our fathers have not kept the word of the Lord; they have not acted in accordance with all that is written in this book. Seek clarification for me from the Lord!"

The men headed for the second district of the city of Jerusalem, to the home of a woman named Huldah, who was highly respected as a prophetess who spoke the word of the Lord.

The woman's face was weathered from age and sorrow, and when she spoke her message, it was direct and to the point. "Tell the man who sent you that this is what the Lord, the God of Israel, says: I am going to bring disaster on this place and its people—all the curses written in the book that has been read in the presence of the king will come to pass. Because the people have forsaken me and burned incense to other gods and provoked me to wrath, my anger will be poured out on this place and not be quenched."

The hearts of the men pounded with fear as Huldah spoke of the wrath of God. But she had a personal message from God as well. She told them that God had seen the king weeping over the sin of the people, and due to Josiah's humble heart and genuine

121

grief, God would hold back his judgment on the people of Israel throughout Josiah's lifetime.

WHEN KING JOSIAH heard the word of the Lord, he made a decision. He called together all the elders of Judah and Jerusalem, all the priests, and all the people from the least to the greatest. Then he went up to the temple of the Lord and stood beside the same pillar where he had been crowned king eighteen years before. Opening the scroll before the people, he read aloud to them from the Book of the Law.

When he had finished reading, he stepped forward. With the people of Israel bearing witness, his clear, strong voice rang out as he renewed the covenant in the presence of the Lord.

"I hereby swear before God to follow the Lord and keep his commands, regulations, and decrees with all my heart and all my soul," he called out, "and to obey the words of the covenant written in this book!"

Stillness followed for a moment until he turned to the people and spoke again, his voice ringing with passion. "Will you join me? Will you pledge to follow after God and to obey his covenants? Will you apply God's word to your lives?"

A cheer rose from the crowd, and the entire congregation of people pledged that day to live in accordance with God's law. There was revival in the land, and great reforms were carried out.

Sorely misused by Josiah's father and grandfather, the temple and the grounds around it not only needed repair but also needed purging. Josiah removed the horses and destroyed the golden chariots used in worship of the sun from inside the temple gate. He tore down the ritual booths where male shrine prostitutes worked in the temple area, and he destroyed the place where women did weaving for the god Asherah. He ordered the removal from the temple of the Lord all the articles made for Baal and

Asherah and the sun, moon, and stars, and burned them in a bonfire outside Jerusalem.

KING JOSIAH REMOVED idols from all the territory belonging to the Israelites, and he encouraged every person in Israel to serve the Lord their God, even going beyond their borders to bring about reform. He instructed the people to celebrate the Passover in Jerusalem on the fourteenth day of the first month, which had not been observed since the days of the prophet Samuel, generations before. As long as Josiah lived, the people did not fail to follow the Lord.

Digging Deeper

Dr. Herbert Lockyer wrote: "Josiah breaks a long, monotonous series of absolutely worthless monarchs. Before and behind him are moral waste and darkness."[2] Given the background he came from, who or what enabled Josiah to emerge a powerful, godly, and influential leader?

There are two accounts of Josiah and his undeniably wicked heritage recorded in the Bible. One is in 2 Kings and the other in 2 Chronicles. (You may read portions of both at the end of this chapter.) Let's take a deeper look into the life and times of Josiah, king of Judah, for greater insight on how this leader broke the mold.

What was Josiah's heritage? Well, he had a pretty scary family tree. His grandfather, Manasseh (not to be confused with Manasseh, the son of Joseph), was given the distinction of being the most evil king of Judah. The Scripture says he became king at age twelve and reigned for fifty-five years. During that time he did evil in the sight of the Lord—things he knew were against God's laws.

Manasseh worshiped the sun, moon, and stars, and defiled the temple of the Lord. He involved himself in witchcraft and sorcery. He built altars to Baal and Asherah and sacrificed his own sons at Topheth, also known as "the Fireplace." The classical scholar Matthew Henry gives some clarity regarding this place of horror.

> There was Topheth, in the valley of the son of Hinnom, very near Jerusalem, where the image of Molech (that god of unnatural cruelty) was kept, to which some sacrificed their children, burning them in the fire. . . . It is supposed to have been called Tophet, from *toph*, a drum, because they beat drums at the burning of the children, that their shrieks might not be heard.[3]

When the Lord spoke to Manasseh and his people, they paid no attention, so God raised up the army of the king of Assyria against them. Manasseh was taken prisoner, and 2 Chronicles 33:11 says that the commander who captured him put a hook in Manasseh's nose, bound him with bronze shackles, and took him to Babylon. Manasseh later humbled himself before God and repented, so God brought him back to Jerusalem, where he attempted to make reforms. Sadly, he was too late to change the heart of his own son.

Amon replaced Manasseh as king upon his death. At age twenty-two, he did the same evil in the sight of the Lord that his father had done. Second Chronicles 33:22 reports that he worshiped and offered sacrifices to all the idols his father had worshiped, which seems to indicate that he sacrificed to Molech at Topheth as well. He must have been hateful to serve, because after only two years as king, his own servants plotted his death and had him assassinated.

Enter Josiah. Amon's firstborn son is crowned king.

How did Josiah break the mold? Josiah was crowned king as a mere child of eight. His inner circle must have included his mother, Jedidah, and other righteous men and women. We don't know much about Jedidah, except that her name means God's darling or "Darling of Jehovah."[4] Also, in the scriptural text, immediately after Jedidah's name, it says of Josiah that "he did what was right in the eyes of the Lord and walked in all the ways of his father David, not turning aside to the right or to the left" (2 Kings 22:2), which seems to indicate that Jedidah gave him some encouragement along his upright path. It is also possible that the prophetess Huldah played a part in his early religious training, and we know that Shaphan, his secretary, was a righteous man.

However, no matter how wonderful his mother or other advisors may have been, Josiah made a decision that altered the course of his life and his nation. He sought after God. His relationship with God brought him under conviction regarding the sins of his fathers and the pagan practices in the land. When the Book of the Law was discovered in the temple ruins, he took great interest first in hearing and then in reading God's law for himself. He then applied the words to his life and his kingdom.

"Josiah is one of the few men in Scripture named before his birth (1 Kings 13:2). He was a chosen vessel, foreordained to fulfill the oracle of the unnamed prophet against the altar . . . at Bethel."[5]

What impact did God's Word have on his life? Scholars agree that the Book of the Law Josiah found was probably the Old Testament book of Deuteronomy. If so, Deuteronomy 4:29 must have resonated in the young king's soul when he heard the words, "But if . . . you seek the Lord your God, you will find him if you look for him with all your heart and with all your soul."

The significance of the "lost and found" Book of the Law was considerable. It contained portions of the law that the Israelites living at that time had never heard before. When the book surfaced Josiah did a number of things: (1) He recognized the value of God's Word. (2) He listened and then read it personally with great interest. (3) He applied its message to his life and to his kingdom and was so convicted that he grieved aloud. (4) He sought clarification from God and received a personal word from the Lord. (5) He shared God's message with all the people and publicly pledged his whole heart in obedience to God. (6) God's Word motivated him to clean house, literally, in the temple, and nationally with regard to idol worship and pagan practices, and he instructed the Israelites to celebrate the Passover for the first time in generations. (7) Josiah challenged his people to live in obedience to God's Word, using his influence to change a nation's practice of idolatry.

Who was Huldah? She was the prophetess whom Josiah's delegation (which included the high priest, his male secretary, and three other men) sought out for a word from the Lord. Note that the Scripture says Josiah sent them "to inquire of the Lord." He did not say, "Go ask Huldah what she thinks." As prophetess she spoke the word of God.

Huldah lived in an area of Jerusalem called the Second Quarter, and scholar Edith Deen writes that "on some maps the Second Quarter is shown to be the section in front of the Temple."[6] She must have been a spiritual woman of great distinction to be sought out by the high priest and emissaries of the king. She spoke the word of the Lord with conviction, and "Huldah's prophecy gave King Josiah greater courage to put into action the laws written in the Book of the Law, which had been sent to her for verification."[7] It was after her counsel that Josiah read the book to the people and pledged to follow God and obey his covenants.

It is interesting to note that Huldah may have been the prophet Jeremiah's aunt. In 2 Kings 22:14 she is described as the wife of Shallum (whose family served the king), and in Jeremiah 32:7 the prophet refers to Shallum as his uncle. Although we know little about this remarkable woman, God used her to influence a young king, and possibly a younger prophet as well. Huldah was a woman so in touch with God that he allowed her to relay his words to others who would in turn influence a nation. (By the way, the Scripture tells of ten women who spoke as prophetesses.[8] There were five in the Old Testament and five in the New Testament.)

What milestones in Josiah's life were recorded in the Bible?

Age eight: Josiah was left fatherless and crowned the king of Judah (2 Kings 22:1).

Age sixteen: In the eighth year of his reign Josiah began to seek a meaningful relationship with God (2 Chron. 34:3).

Age twenty: In the twelfth year of his reign he began to purge the kingdom of idols, pagan altars, sorcery, and witchcraft (2 Chron. 34:3).

Age twenty-six: In the eighteenth year of his reign he began the repair and restoration of the temple and pledged himself to follow the Lord and his commands with all his heart and soul. That same year he celebrated the Passover to the Lord in Jerusalem (2 Chron. 34:8–35:1).

Age thirty-nine: In the thirty-first year of his reign, he was shot in battle by an archer. All Judah and Jerusalem mourned for him. The year was 609 BC.[9]

How can this story apply to your life?

Allow God's Word to change your life. The Bible has the power to teach, convict, rebuke, inspire, encourage, motivate, and much, much more. It struck me in reading Josiah's story and the dramatic application of God's Word to his life that I sometimes read the Bible without making it personal—without applying it personally—which effectively renders the powerful message null and void in my life. After reading about Josiah, how do you think God would like to change your life?

Humble yourself before God and confess any known sin in your life. After hearing God's word from the lost book, Josiah was so convicted that he grieved and tore his robes. Then he sought to make things right. Do you experience sorrow when thinking of the wrong choices in your past? Have you told God how you feel about it?

With God's help, identify and eliminate the idols in your life. What idols? Josiah recognized that his nation would never experience the blessings of God as long as they continued to flirt with false gods. Are there any idols in your life?

> Christians in modern cultures often think of idolatry as quaint ancient curiosity or a superstitious practice found only among primitive peoples. Wrong! Idolatry thrives today in the most sophisticated societies on earth. An idol is anything or anyone that comes to take the place of God in our lives.[10]

That "something" could be our job or a relationship, a habit, the television, or an activity or skill that we spend hours doing rather than taking time to spend with God in his holy Word.

Ask God to help you to identify any idols in your life, and make your relationship with him a priority.

Recognize that one person's faith can affect many others. Josiah took time to seek God's face and then made the decision to use his position to influence thousands of other lives. Who do you influence? Think about your family, friends, neighbors, and the people you work with. Does the life you lead in front of them encourage them in their relationship with God as well?

God used Josiah within his sphere of influence, and he can use you within yours as well. To do this effectively, you need to follow Josiah's example and turn your heart toward God. Remember to humble yourself and remain teachable, being willing to "clean house" and getting rid of the things that keep you from spending time with God. When your heart is right, don't be afraid to share your testimony with others. It may inspire them to seek out a personal relationship with God, through his Son, Jesus Christ, as well.

THE DEAD SEA SCROLL exhibit was coming to west Michigan! It was the most media-hyped exhibit ever to come to the Public Museum of Grand Rapids, and Graydon and I, as part of the general public, started reading and hearing about it months before the exhibit arrived. Owned by the Israel Antiquities Authority and rarely displayed outside of Israel, the rare and valuable exhibit would attract thousands of visitors from every walk of life to west Michigan over the three and a half month period it was on display.

My husband came home from work one day with an engraved invitation from a large law firm inviting us to come and view the exhibit as their guests, and to attend a formal evening reception that would be held at the museum the first week of the exhibit. I was thrilled. We had both wanted to see the exhibit anyway, and I happened to be researching and writing about a biblical character named Josiah. I wanted to look at the ancient writings and imagine what it must have been like for Josiah to discover a scroll containing the Word of the Lord that had been lost for generations.

On the night we were to attend, I stuffed a small tablet and a pen in my evening bag so I could take notes, and off we went. At the museum, security was high, and each guest had to step through a metal detector and have their bags searched. Inside, people milled around everywhere, eating, sipping drinks, and socializing. We could see that a line was forming at the top of the stairs for the exhibit, so after greeting a few people here and there, we headed for the line.

As we entered the exhibit, we found ourselves stepping into a cave in the Judean Desert. The simulation with old pottery pieces and an audio introduction to the display ended at a small theater, where a video presentation gave some background on the discovery of the scrolls. A Bedouin shepherd boy, searching for a stray goat, accidentally discovered the first of the scrolls in a long-abandoned cave in 1947. How little did the boy realize that his discovery would lead to an amazing treasure, the Dead Sea Scrolls, which are a collection of ancient religious writings that date from the third century BC to approximately AD 68. Since that first discovery, over one hundred thousand fragments have been found and painstakingly pieced together into over nine hundred different documents.

Especially significant to Jews and Christians is the fact that approximately two hundred of the nine hundred documents are biblical writings that represent the oldest known text of the Hebrew Bible, including every book except the book of Esther. Also significant is the fact that the ancient writings have essentially the same content as the Old Testament portion of the Bible we still use today.

As we moved from display to display, we learned about the scribes from the Qumran community that had carefully copied the Hebrew text onto scrolls and then hid them in nearby desert caves when Roman troops invaded their community on their way to destroy Jerusalem.

Later, as we lingered in the display area, I found myself looking around at the other guests, wondering what the exhibit meant to them. For some, I'm sure it was simply a curiosity. For others it was a collection of rare and valuable papers. For me, it affirmed that the Bible I read today is accurate according to the oldest manuscripts.

Graydon and I were thoughtful as we drove the hour home. "So what intense thoughts are churning in that head of yours tonight?" my husband asked with a smile.

"Well, we've just viewed what some people consider to be the greatest archaeological discovery of modern times," I began, "but it's only fragments of history unless people who read it take God at his word and apply it to their daily lives. I'm just wondering how many people will pick up a Bible for themselves after being here tonight. I just wonder."

A Whispered Prayer

Dear Heavenly Father, so often I've neglected your Word to the point that it might as well have been a lost book. Please forgive me for not seeking you with my whole heart, and help me to discover the truths of the Bible personally and to apply them to my life. Lord, please help me to identify the things that are a hindrance to my relationship with you, and help me use my own sphere of influence to touch the lives of others with your love and forgiveness. In the precious name of Jesus, Amen.

Get Up and Go Ideas for Tomorrow

1. I will ask God to help me identify idols in my life that interfere with my relationship with him, and with his help, I will take steps to eliminate them.
2. I will tell someone else about my faith in God and his Son, Jesus Christ, and use my influence to encourage him or her to seek after a relationship with God as well.

A Thought to Ponder as I Fall Asleep

Do I allow God's Word to impact my life? What happened the last time it did?

The Scripture Reading: 2 Kings 21:17–24, 22:1–2; 2 Chronicles 34:3–12, 14–33; 35:18; 2 Kings 23:4, 10, 24–25

As for the other events of Manasseh's reign, and all he did, including the sin he committed, are they not written in the book of the annals of the kings of Judah? Manasseh rested with his fathers and was buried in his palace garden, the garden of Uzza. And Amon his son succeeded him as king.

Amon was twenty-two years old when he became king, and he reigned in Jerusalem two years. His mother's name was Meshullemeth daughter of Haruz; she was from Jotbah. He did evil in the eyes of the LORD, as his father Manasseh had done. He walked in all the ways of his father; he worshiped the idols his father had worshiped, and bowed down to them. He forsook the LORD, the God of his fathers, and did not walk in the way of the LORD.

Amon's officials conspired against him and assassinated the king in his palace. Then the people of the land killed all who had plotted against King Amon, and they made Josiah his son king in his place....

Josiah was eight years old when he became king, and he reigned in Jerusalem thirty-one years. His mother's name was Jedidah daughter of Adaiah; she was from Bozkath. He did what was right in the eyes of the LORD and walked in all the ways of his [fore]father David, not turning aside to the right or to the left....

In the eighth year of his reign, while he was still young, he began to seek the God of his [fore]father David. In his twelfth year he began to purge Judah and Jerusalem of high places, Asherah poles, carved idols and cast images. Under his direction the altars of the Baals were torn down; he cut to pieces the incense altars that were above them, and smashed the Asherah poles, the idols and the images. These he broke to pieces and scattered over the graves of those who had sacrificed to them. He burned the bones of the priests on their altars, and so he purged Judah and Jerusalem. In the towns of Manasseh, Ephraim and Simeon, as far as Naphtali, and in the ruins around them, he tore down the altars and the Asherah poles and crushed the idols to powder and cut to pieces all the incense altars throughout Israel. Then he went back to Jerusalem.

In the eighteenth year of Josiah's reign, to purify the land and the temple, he sent Shaphan son of Azaliah and Maaseiah the ruler of the city, with Joah son of Joahaz, the recorder, to repair the temple of the LORD his God.

They went to Hilkiah the high priest and gave him the money that had been brought into the temple of God, which the Levites who were the doorkeepers had collected from the people.... Then they entrusted it to the men appointed to supervise the work on the LORD's temple. These men paid the workers who repaired and restored the temple. They also gave money to the carpenters and builders to purchase dressed stone, and timber for joists and beams for the buildings that the kings of Judah had allowed to fall into ruin.

The men did the work faithfully....

While they were bringing out the money that had been taken into the temple of the LORD, Hilkiah the priest found the Book of the Law of the LORD that had been given through Moses. Hilkiah said to Shaphan the secretary, "I have found the Book of the Law in the temple of the LORD." He gave it to Shaphan.

Then Shaphan took the book to the king and reported to him: "Your officials are doing everything that has been committed to them. They have paid out the money that was in the temple of the LORD and have entrusted it to the supervisors and workers." Then Shaphan the secretary informed the king, "Hilkiah the priest has given me a book." And Shaphan read from it in the presence of the king.

When the king heard the words of the Law, he tore his robes. He gave these orders to Hilkiah, Ahikam son of Shaphan, Abdon son of Micah, Shaphan the secretary and Asaiah the king's attendant: "Go and inquire of the LORD for me and for the remnant in Israel and Judah about what is written in this book that has been found. Great is the LORD's anger that is poured out on us because our fathers have not kept the word of the LORD; they have not acted in accordance with all that is written in this book."

Hilkiah and those the king had sent with him went to speak to the prophetess Huldah, who was the wife of Shallum son of Tokhath, the son of Hasrah, keeper of the wardrobe. She lived in Jerusalem, in the Second District.

She said to them, "This is what the LORD, the God of Israel, says: Tell the man who sent you to me, 'This is what the LORD says: I am going to bring disaster on this place and its people—all the curses written in the book that has been read in the presence of the king of Judah. Because they have forsaken me and burned incense to other gods and provoked me to anger by all that their hands have made, my anger will be poured out on this place and will not be quenched.' Tell the king of Judah, who sent you to inquire of the LORD, 'This is what the LORD, the God of Israel, says concerning the words you heard: Because your heart was responsive and you humbled yourself before God when you heard what he spoke against this place and its people, and because you humbled yourself before me and tore your robes and wept in my presence, I have heard you, declares the LORD. Now I will gather you to your fathers, and you will be buried in peace. Your eyes will not see all the disaster I am going to bring on this place and on those who live here.'"

So they took her answer back to the king.

Then the king called together all the elders of Judah and Jerusalem. He went up to the temple of the LORD with the men of Judah, the people of Jerusalem, the priests and the Levites—all the people from the least to the greatest. He read in their hearing all the words of the Book of the Covenant, which had been found in the temple of the LORD. The king stood by his pillar and renewed the covenant in the presence of the LORD—to follow the LORD and keep his commands, regulations and decrees with all his heart and all his soul, and to obey the words of the covenant written in this book.

Then he had everyone in Jerusalem and Benjamin pledge themselves to it; the people of Jerusalem did this in accordance with the covenant of God, the God of their fathers.

Josiah removed all the detestable idols from all the territory belonging to the Israelites, and he had all who were present in Israel serve the LORD their God. As long as he lived, they did not fail to follow the LORD, the God of their fathers.

Josiah celebrated the Passover to the LORD in Jerusalem....

The king ordered Hilkiah the high priest, the priests next in rank and the doorkeepers to remove from the temple of the LORD all the articles made for Baal and Asherah and all the starry hosts. He burned them outside Jerusalem in the fields of the Kidron Valley and took the ashes to Bethel....

He desecrated Topheth, which was in the Valley of Ben Hinnom, so no one could use it to sacrifice his son or daughter in the fire to Molech....

Furthermore, Josiah got rid of the mediums and spiritists, the household gods, the idols and all the other detestable things seen in Judah and Jerusalem. This he did to fulfill the requirements of the law written in the book that Hilkiah the priest had discovered in the temple of the LORD. Neither before nor after Josiah was there a king like him who turned to the LORD as he did—with all his heart and with all his soul and with all his strength, in accordance with all the Law of Moses.

Final Note: King Josiah reigned as king of Judah from 641–609 BC.[11] The histories of Josiah and his wicked father and grandfather are recorded in both 2 Kings 21–23 and 2 Chronicles 33–35.

Mixed Blessings

A Story about Honor, Sacrifice, and an Unplanned Pregnancy

The house was a flurry of wedding preparations. Five brides-maids had been fitted for their gowns, tuxedos had been ordered, the invitations had been sent out weeks before, and my wedding gown hung in beaded splendor from the top of the closet door frame in my bedroom.

I had worked in a city three hours away that summer and had come back home just a few weeks before the wedding to help with final preparations. Lying on my bed in the familiar comfort of that bedroom, I imagined my wedding day—and my wedding night. I was nineteen years old and a college sophomore, and I was a virgin.

In two weeks I would marry Graydon Dimkoff, a twenty-three-year-old law student, and we were eager to begin our life together as man and wife. We had consciously decided to remain sexually pure before marriage, and that restraint had created a sweet and exciting anticipation of our wedding night.

Then something unexpected happened.

Several weeks before, I had discovered a lump in my breast. Overwhelmed with my job and wedding plans, I put the matter out of my mind. When I came home and mentioned it to my mom, she immediately took me to the doctor. From there we were sent to a specialist who scheduled surgery for four days later—just ten days before my wedding.

Suddenly, my excitement was overshadowed by the threat of breast cancer. My thoughts were chaotic. Wasn't I far too young for that disease? Was this life threatening? If not, would my body be disfigured? Would I ever be able to nurse a child? The anticipation of being intimate with my husband suddenly dissipated. I knew Graydon loved me, but if I were to lose a breast, would he still desire me? Although he insisted that his love was unconditional, the silky, scented nightwear already packed for our honeymoon suddenly seemed far too transparent. I poured out my heart to my heavenly Father.

Oh, God, please help me! This is supposed to be the happiest time in my life, and suddenly I feel like I'm coming apart inside. I want your will for my life, but I need your peace so desperately! Will you help Graydon too as we face the week ahead, and when we make decisions for the future after that? I believe you brought us together, and I am choosing to entrust my situation and our future to your care. Help me to rest in your love for both of us tonight.

The following Sunday evening the "Afman girls" were the special music at church, and as I sang with my sisters I felt choked with emotion. Following the service, my dad, who was the pastor, closed in prayer. Then, clearing his throat, he made an announcement. "You are all aware that we have a wedding coming up shortly in our family. We also have a challenge facing us on Tuesday morning, as Jennie will be undergoing surgery for a suspicious lump in her breast."

My shocked eyes met his, and Dad's voice broke for a moment as he went on. "I'd like to ask Jennie to come to the front, and to invite those who would care to stay after to join us here in prayer."

That night, I knelt at the front of the church, and precious friends gently touched my head and prayed. In the midst of one of the most chaotic weeks of my life, peace came over me.

On Tuesday, I awoke in a recovery room to learn that the doctor had removed a benign tumor the size of a walnut. I was a healthy young woman, and our wedding plans could go ahead as scheduled! With grateful hearts Graydon and I celebrated our wedding day, and that night I was wooed by a gentle lover, who insisted with a charming grin that the Band-Aid I still wore only enhanced my attractions! We would later thank God for allowing us that precious time together.

WEDDINGS ARE A CAUSE for celebration and rejoicing, but there is usually some stress that factors in as well—even without having to deal with unexpected emergencies! Recalling the details of my own situation caused me to consider with fresh wonder an amazing story in Scripture about another engaged couple who received unexpected news before their wedding. The bride was a teenager named Mary, and her groom was a carpenter named Joseph. Without a doubt, God brought them together for a special purpose.

Mary and Joseph's Story

The girl hummed as she carried the water from the well, her face breaking into a smile as she passed over the threshold. Greeting her mother, she poured some of the water into a basin to wash the dust from her face, arms, and feet. The older woman couldn't help but smile at her daughter's fresh face sparkling with excitement. *And why not,* she thought to herself, *the girl is newly betrothed, and her handsome husband-to-be is coming for supper tonight. Our Mary is getting a good man. Joseph is kind, reliable, and most important, he honors God with his life, just as our Mary does.*

"Come wash and sort these figs, Mary," her mother instructed, "while I pit the olives to stuff in the flat bread."

"Yes, Mama," Mary replied, reaching for the basket. "I saw Roman soldiers in the village again when I went to the well for water. Why do they come so often to Nazareth?"

"They are everywhere, child. To hear your father talk, the Roman government will crush us with heavy taxation and political oppression." She sighed. "How I long for the Messiah, the anointed one the prophets of old promised, who will establish a new kingdom and rule the world with justice."

"Did you ever wish to bear the Messiah, Mama?" Mary asked thoughtfully.

"Of course!" came the ready reply. "Every generation of Jewish women has lived in hope of that great honor. To bear the Messiah would be blessing indeed!"

As mother and daughter continued to work, the conversation made its way to a familiar topic, the upcoming wedding. "I hope that Cousin Elizabeth and her husband, Zechariah, will be able to come," Mary said as she sorted the figs. "I so want her to be here!"

"Don't set your heart on them coming, Mary," her mother advised. "They are both elderly, and the long journey from the Judean hill country may be too much for them. But I agree that it would be wonderful if they could be here. You have always been special to Elizabeth, since she never had children of her own."

"I love to visit her, Mama, and she's taught me so much about knowing God and about the ordinances of the Lord. I enjoy watching her interact with Zechariah too. That's how I hope my marriage will be." Mary sighed. "Their love for each other is so obvious, and even though Elizabeth is barren, Zechariah has stayed faithful to her."

Mary's mother smiled fondly at her. "As I'm sure Joseph will be to you. Now hurry on with those figs. Joseph will be arriving here for dinner soon."

THAT NIGHT AFTER SUPPER with Mary's family, Joseph headed for home with a light heart; he couldn't help whistling as he went on his way. Mary had seemed to like the gift he had brought her, and the memory gave him great pleasure. His normal carpentry job found him sawing logs and making ox yokes or sturdy door frames, but he had made the time to craft a small, fragrant cedar box and carve the cover with the outline of a lamb. He had wondered if a floral design wouldn't be more appropriate, but her delight had warmed his heart like the sun on his face on a cool spring day. *Thank you, God, for Mary*, his heart sang. *She is precious to me, and I will love her and care for her all of my life.*

AFTER JOSEPH LEFT and the dishes were cleared away, Mary told her parents good night, took her sleeping pallet, and headed for the narrow stairway that ran alongside the house and led to the flat roof. The thought of sleeping under the starry sky in the warm night air was compelling.

139

Reaching the roof, Mary lifted her face to the heavens and thanked God for his many blessings. She felt very small under so vast a sky.

"Hello, Mary. You may feel insignificant, but the Lord is with you, and he sees you as very special!"

Startled, Mary's eyes flew open, and she stumbled back a step. A bright and shining being stood shimmering before her. *He knows my name! What's happening here?*

"Don't be afraid, Mary," the being went on gently. "I am the angel Gabriel, and God has sent me with a very special message this night." He smiled, and a quiet calm came over Mary as she listened. "Mary, you have found favor with God. You will soon become pregnant with a son, and you are to give him the name Jesus." Gabriel's voice lifted joyfully. "He will be great and will be called the Son of the Most High. The Lord God will give him the throne of his father David, and his kingdom will never end. Dear Mary, chosen of the Lord—you will bear the Messiah!"

MARY BELIEVED. Her heart was pounding furiously, but a curious joy began filling her soul, and she knew without doubt that what the glistening angel said was true. But she couldn't keep the practical question from slipping from her mouth. "How will this happen, since I am a virgin?"

The angel smiled and explained the mystery as best he could. "The Holy Spirit will come upon you, Mary, and the power of the Most High will overshadow you. The Holy One that will be born to you will be called the Son of God." Then, noting the furrow of concentration lining her brow, he added with a grin, "And I have other good news as well. Your relative Elizabeth is going to have a child too—even in her old age!"

When Mary's mouth dropped open at the news, Gabriel's smile became broader. "She is already six months along."

Tears of joy filled Mary's eyes.

"Nothing is impossible with God, Mary," Gabriel added quietly.

Inhaling the cool night air, Mary smiled back at Gabriel for a moment and then humbly bowed her head. "I am the Lord's servant," she said to him. "May these things happen to me as you have said."

When she lifted her head, the angel was gone.

Waking early the next morning, Mary involuntarily placed her hands over the flat plane of her stomach. "I must go to see Elizabeth!" she said out loud, jumping up and gathering her pallet.

MOTHER AND DAUGHTER had a long talk that morning. First doubtful, her mother insisted that Mary must have had a strange dream.

"No, Mother, it was no dream. I will bear the Messiah!" Clasping her mother's hands, Mary studied the lined face of the woman who had bore her. "I have no doubt that when I return from Elizabeth's with news of her pregnancy, you too will know the wonderful truth! Don't be afraid, and don't worry about what will happen in the future. For now, it is enough for me to know that I am to bear God's Son. You talk to Father about this while I am gone. When I come back from Elizabeth's, my own pregnancy will be apparent, and we'll deal with the betrothal at that time. Don't cry, Mother! Of course I'm afraid, but my joy is far greater than my fear!"

Packing quickly for her journey, Mary paused to pick up the small cedar box Joseph had made for her. Tracing her finger over the intricate carving of the lamb, she sighed and whispered a prayer. *Oh, God, please help Joseph to understand.*

How Mary looked forward to being with Elizabeth! The three days' journey between their homes made the rare visits precious to both women, but never had Mary been more anxious to see her friend.[1]

When she entered their home, Mary saw the door to the garden open and Elizabeth herself, round with child, standing on the doorstep. "Elizabeth!" Mary called, joyfully rushing to meet her.

Upon hearing her voice, Elizabeth suddenly clutched her stomach. "Oh, Mary! Blessed are you among women, and blessed is the child you will bear! Why am I so favored, that the mother of my Lord should come to visit me?" Tears of joy started down the weathered face of the older woman as she embraced Mary. "When I heard your voice in the garden, I felt my baby leap inside me."

Mary wept and hugged Elizabeth tightly. Later she learned that Gabriel had also visited Zechariah and told him that his wife would bear a child. Because Zechariah had doubted that this might happen, the angel had told him he would be speechless until the child was born.

"Things are quiet but so very happy in our house these days, dear Mary," Elizabeth said. "But it's good to have someone to talk to me!"

Mary had a wonderful three-month visit with her cousin, but soon it was time to return home to Joseph.

"What?" Joseph stared at Mary in disbelief as she stood quietly before him. "Your father told me you had something of grave importance to tell me, but I envisioned some illness . . ."

"Oh, Joseph, if only you could have heard what the angel said to me," Mary said earnestly.

"Mary, stop with the angel story!" Joseph rubbed his hands over his eyes, wishing he could erase the reality of Mary's pregnancy away. "I have to think about what to do." He turned away without meeting her eyes. "I have to think."

JOSEPH SPENT THE NIGHT tossing and turning on his pallet, his emotions running the gamut from anger to sorrow. To think that Mary had been unfaithful tormented him to the point of despair. And then, that she stood there pregnant and said she had never been with a man! Thoughts of the home he had so lovingly prepared while she had been gone mocked him. He snorted, remembering how excited he had been to show her the sturdy table and bench he had finished in her absence. What a fool he had been!

But he loved her still. A tear slipped down his tanned cheek, and he wiped it away with a calloused knuckle. What could he do? He could no longer marry her, but no matter what she had done, he couldn't bear to see her publicly punished for adultery. His eyes squeezed shut at the thought of her slight form being battered by rocks. He shuddered. No, he couldn't let that happen.

The thought came to him that he should meet with her father and arrange for a private decree of divorcement. Perhaps if she left town again to stay with her cousin, she would be protected. Talk and speculation would eventually die down—and he wouldn't have to see her in the village, growing round with a child that was not his own.

After coming to this conclusion, Joseph fell into a troubled sleep.

Suddenly a voice spoke to him. "Joseph, son of David. Do not be afraid to take Mary home as your wife."

Was he dreaming? He must be. But the voice seemed so real, so clear.

The voice continued. "What is conceived in her is from the Holy Spirit. She will give birth to a son, and you are to give him the name Jesus, because he will save his people from their sins."

When Joseph woke up, he stared calmly at the ceiling above him. The contorted jumble of emotions he had struggled with the night before was gone. His mission was clear, and joy began welling up inside of him. *Mary! My precious Mary has been chosen to bear the Messiah! And I, Joseph, unworthy as I am, am honored to name the child of God!* He laughed out loud. *The Messiah is coming!*

THEY MARRIED SOONER than planned, and without fanfare. Many in the village were surprised but assumed it was the poverty of Mary's family that kept things quiet.

Inside the home of Joseph a sweet but unconsummated marriage was established. Joseph's joy over Mary's pregnancy made her love him all the more, and the miracle baby was a precious secret they guarded carefully. As the months passed and Mary's body became swollen with the unborn child, their excitement only grew. Then, unsettling news came regarding a government census.

Placing a plate of bread, cheese, and lentils before her husband, Mary lowered her cumbersome body to the short bench across from him. "Are you sure about this, Joseph? There's no postponing the trip?"

"I wish it weren't true," he responded, clearly frustrated. "Caesar Augustus has ordered that a census be taken of the entire Roman world. We're ordered to register in the town of our family's origin, and since I belong to the house and line of David, we've got to travel to Bethlehem. It's about ninety miles," he added soberly.[2] "Will you be able to make it?"

As she studied her husband's concerned face, Mary felt her worries subside. "God knows about the census, and he certainly knows about this baby, so I think I'll be fine," she said with a smile. "I'll bake extra bread tomorrow for the trip." She rubbed her swollen belly. "I'd better pack swaddling cloths for this little one, who may not wait until we get back home to be born."

TRAVEL WAS FAR SLOWER than anticipated as people crowded the roadway leading to Bethlehem. The donkey Joseph had secured for Mary to ride was better than walking, but by the second day on the road her back was screaming with pain. When they stopped at night, she sometimes wept with relief. As for Joseph, he cared for her as tenderly as he could, lifting the goatskin to provide a drink of water and gently massaging the small of her back.

"Hold on, Mary," he urged, stifling his own worry. "Soon you'll be in the comfort and privacy of an inn."

NIGHT WAS FALLING when they finally approached the city of Bethlehem. Seeing the lights of an inn up ahead lightened his heart, and he quickened his step, calling out encouragement to Mary behind him. Tugging on the harness, he urged the donkey to hurry.

Joseph saw the baggage piled up near the entrance, and an uneasy feeling came over him again. He knocked on the door several times. No one answered. *I'm not about to give up*, he thought. *Not with Mary in labor.* He pounded on the door again.

When the disheveled innkeeper finally came to the door, he seemed annoyed. "No room, man! Didn't you see the sign? We're packed to the gills tonight." He started to shut the door, but a groan of pain from the darkness behind Joseph caught the man's attention. "What was that?"

"Sir! It's my wife, she needs shelter. Please, sir," Joseph begged as the man moved to close the door. "She's about to have a baby."

Another cry pierced the darkness. "Joseph, help me!" Mary cried out. "I must get down from this donkey."

As Joseph turned to help Mary, the innkeeper's gruff tone softened a bit. "Well, take her around back to the stable. Your wife will be out of the wind, and she'll have some privacy there." He cleared his throat awkwardly. "I'll leave you two to your business," he muttered as he closed the door.

THE STABLE WAS BUILT into the side of the hill behind the inn. Between powerful contractions, Mary's eyes only vaguely focused on her surroundings. She was just grateful for the clean bed of hay she was resting on, and for Joseph—dear Joseph, who hadn't bargained for any of this when he'd arranged to marry her.

AFTER HANGING HIS LANTERN from an upper beam near Mary's feet, Joseph raised his forearm to wipe the sweat from his brow. Then he bent to dip a rag in the bucket of water and wipe it gently over Mary's flushed face.

The air smelled of manure. *Manure*, he thought, shaking his head and struggling with a feeling of failure. *What a place for the King of kings to be born. When God made me Mary's guardian, did he expect more from me than this?*

When Mary clutched his hand in a death grip, Joseph raised his eyes to survey their accommodations. Harnesses hung from pegs on the wall, and an ox yoke leaned against the rails of a stall.

"I need to push, Joseph," Mary gasped. "Now! Maybe it would help if I tried to squat. You get in front and help the baby!"

She cried out loud as she pushed, and Joseph groaned with her. Her water broke. When he saw the baby's head, he cheered her on. She pushed again, gulping for breath between contractions. After the final push and another gush of water and blood, Joseph's large, rough hands tenderly guided the infant into the world. Gently he wiped mucus away from the baby's nose and mouth while Mary expelled the afterbirth.

When the child sucked air into his tiny lungs and let out a wail, both Mary and Joseph laughed for joy. A few moments later, Joseph took a piece of string and tied a knot around the umbilical cord before cutting the slippery appendage with a trembling hand. Then, laying the baby against his wife's breast, Joseph gently covered them and bent to kiss Mary's smiling, tear-stained face.

Grabbing the bucket, he headed to the well for fresh water. Upon his return, he cleared away the wet blankets, forked fresh straw in place of the soiled, and stepped outside again to give Mary some privacy so she could wash herself and the child.

Under the star-studded sky, Joseph inhaled deeply and found his cheeks wet with tears. *Thank you, God, for the gift of your Son*, his heart sang. Then more sober thoughts came. *Who am I to raise your Son, Lord? Please help me to do it right.*

When he returned to them, he found a scene that would forever be etched in his memory. Mary had washed the child, wrapped him firmly in strips of swaddling cloth, and then improvised a cradle. On a soft blanket in the crude, hay-filled manger lay the newborn King. Mary was kneeling next to him, studying his face with a look of wonder.

When Joseph knelt beside her, Mary leaned her head wearily against his shoulder. He knew she should sleep, but the miracle was too fresh, and neither felt like moving for a while.

THEY HAD BOTH DOZED off when the sound of hushed voices woke Joseph. To his surprise, a scruffy group of shepherds were gathered outside the stable, trying to peer inside. Instantly on guard, Joseph blocked their way and inquired as to their business.

The men were excited, and several tried to speak at once. "We were watching our flocks in the hills near here when an angel appeared to us!" began one. "The glory of the Lord was so bright around him that we shrank back in fear!" said another. Then a young boy spoke up.

"But the angel told us not to be afraid, and he said, 'I bring you wonderful news that will bring great joy to many people!'"

An older man placed his hand on the boy's shoulder. "Is the Messiah here? The angel said that today, in the city of David, a Savior has been born, and that he is Christ the Lord! He said we would find him lying in a manger. Have we come to the right place?" he asked earnestly.

Realizing the men were no threat, and that instead, they had been sent by God, Joseph asked them to wait a moment while he went inside.

"Mary," he said, gently nudging his wife's shoulder. "We have visitors. They've come to see the baby."

Mary opened her sleep-filled eyes to see the entrance to the stable filled with strangers who were looking at her baby in the manger. To her amazement, they knelt reverently before him.

"Tell the child's mother what you've seen this night," Joseph told the men.

The men repeated their story and went on to say that the entire sky behind the angel had lit up with other angels, and that the heavens had rung with their joyful song of praise. *"Glory to God in the highest, and on earth, peace to men on whom his favor rests!"*

"When the angels disappeared into the heavens, we left immediately to find the child!" the youngest shepherd finished.

"And I am so glad you did," Mary said kindly, her heart almost bursting with joy. "You are the very first to see the Savior!"

After they'd gone, Mary and Joseph looked at each other in wonder. "God announced this baby's birth with a choir of angels," she said, still amazed by the shepherds' story. "Imagine that!"

"What a night!" Joseph whispered.

A weary smile lit Mary's face in return. "I will remember this for as long as I live, Joseph. Aren't you glad that we dared to say yes to God's will for our lives?"

Digging Deeper

After the birth, earthly ministry, death, resurrection, and ascension of Jesus into heaven, many stories were told about what had happened. Luke, a physician, historian, and traveling companion of the apostle Paul, was led by the Holy Spirit to interview those who were eyewitnesses so that he could record an "orderly account" of those events.

I found it interesting to note that several scholars believe it was entirely possible that Luke personally interviewed Mary, the mother of Jesus, because the account of the nativity is so detailed. Matthew also wrote about the birth of Jesus, and in the next chapter of *More Night Whispers*, our story picks up with the events that followed the baby's birth, including Matthew's account of the Magi, or wise men.

Let's look deeper into several aspects of this wonderful story.

Betrothal was serious business. Once entered into between a girl's parents and the groom or his representative, a betrothal could only be broken through a decree of divorcement. If a woman had sexual relations prior to marriage, she could be stoned on grounds of adultery. During the betrothal, which could last up to a year, the home would be prepared by the groom, the wedding clothes would be prepared by the bride, and the bride's family would plan the wedding festivities.[3]

I was glad to find in my research that the bride was somewhat involved in the betrothal process. "In New Testament times a man such as Joseph became formally betrothed when he gave a present to the girl and said, 'By this, thou are set apart for me according to the laws of Moses and of Israel.'"[4] The deal was sealed with a gift for the bride. In our story, I pictured Joseph, the carpenter, crafting this gift with his own hands.

The greatest honor came with great complications. When shocked by the appearance and astounding message of the angel Gabriel, Mary didn't ask, "But what will Joseph think?" She didn't bring up the fact that she might be cast out of her community, called a harlot, or even stoned. Instead, her faith was so great that she accepted this honor by responding, "I am the Lord's servant. May it be to me as you have said" (Luke 1:38). She willingly surrendered the control of her body, her life, and her future to God.

Mary had a heritage of faith. We don't know much about Mary's parents except that they lived in the poor village of Nazareth and they raised a daughter who was full of faith and found great favor with God. We also know they arranged for her to marry Joseph, a godly man.

However, we are told something in Scripture about her relatives, Zechariah and Elizabeth (Luke 1:5–80). Who were they? Zechariah was a priest, and Elizabeth was the daughter of a family of priests of the house of Aaron. They were elderly and had been married and childless for many years. The Scripture says both of them were upright in the sight of God and obeyed all of his commandments. God chose to bless this couple in their old age with the birth of a baby who would become an evangelist and proclaim the coming ministry of the Messiah. Zechariah and Elizabeth's child's name was John, later known as John the Baptist or Baptizer.

I found myself thankful for Mary's sake that the angel told her that Elizabeth would also give birth to a child, and that nothing was impossible with God. To have the counsel of the older, familiar, and godly Elizabeth during this overwhelming transition must have brought great comfort, encouragement, and validation to young Mary.

Who gets the "Most Wonderful Husband in History" award? The award has to go to Joseph. He was a remarkable man, and his love for Mary must have been genuine, because even when he thought Mary had betrayed him, he wanted to protect her. Ralph Gower, in his helpful *The New Manners and Customs of Bible Times*, had this to say:

> Joseph did not want to expose her publicly, because as a supposed adulteress, Mary would have been stoned to death. It must have taken a great deal of love for Mary and a great deal of trust in God speaking through his dream that enabled Joseph to marry her. Maybe this is a reflection of the character God looked for in the man who was to bring up Jesus.[5]

A man of compassion and great faith, Joseph followed God's directives and cared for a young woman who was heavy with a child not his own, and later was willing to leave the country to protect that child. God spoke to Joseph in dreams, explaining each situation, warning of impending danger, and directing his faithful steps.

Natural Childbirth 101. Mary gave birth to the Christ child far from her own bed and without the attention of her mother, a midwife, or the comforts of home. The ninety mile journey from Nazareth to Bethlehem had taken many days, and Mary delivered soon after they reached the city.[6] The new mother gave birth in a stable with her husband (with whom she had not yet been intimate) assisting her in very personal ways. After the birth, an exhausted but joyful Mary tenderly washed and wrapped the baby in swaddling cloths, which weren't exactly diapers. "To swaddle a child was to wrap an infant in strips of cloth, much like narrow bandages. This was believed to ensure the correct early development of the limbs."[7]

It is easy to imagine the joy of new parents as they hold their first child, but imagine the awe involved for this couple at the birth of Jesus—a miracle child, the Son of God! Then to their surprise and affirmation, God sent out two amazing birth announcements. The heavens broke open as angels joyfully proclaimed the birth to humble shepherds in the hills nearby. And a star would eventually lead wise men from the East to worship and honor the newborn. How affirming and exciting these events must have been to the humble and obedient newlyweds.

How can this story apply to your life?

Recognize the baby Jesus for who he really is—the Son of God, the Messiah. Although Luke took great pains to interview eyewitnesses and accurately record the events that unfolded in this story, his careful documentation has little meaning unless we accept by faith the validity and truth of who Jesus is.

I've tried to imagine what it will be like to die and wake up in heaven, where there is no pain, fear, heartache, oppression, despair, poverty, or sickness, and instead peace, beauty, and joy. But can you imagine being God, leaving all that behind and waking up to the smell of manure, being bound by a tiny, helpless body in a world full of grief? That is exactly what Jesus was willing to do for us. He was willing to live life from our point of view at a very humble level, to be hunted and ridiculed, to suffer scorn, and to pay the ultimate price for our sin by his death on the cross.

Care more about your relationship with God than about the opinion of others. Mary faithfully followed the will of God in her life, in spite of the fact that it was inconvenient and didn't seem a good fit with important plans she had already made. Do you dare to say yes to God's will for your life? When we choose to be obedient to the call that God lays on our hearts, he will work out the details. What is required of us is to trust him and to obey. "Blessed is she who has believed that what the Lord has said to her will be accomplished" (Luke 1:45).

If you have children, encourage them to seek God's will for their lives. Scripture tells us nothing about Mary's parents, but in contemplating Mary's mother and what she must have been like, I think she must have seen something special in her daughter and encouraged her to seek God's will for her life.

In thinking of Mary's mom, I was reminded of my own mom and a letter she wrote to me the night before my wedding.

My Dearest Jennie,

Tomorrow at this time you will no longer be Jennie Afman, but rather, Jennie Dimkoff. Where have the years gone? They have slipped away too quickly.

Before I became pregnant with you, I longed for another baby. Dad thought we should wait because he was in Bible school, but he finally came around to my way of thinking.

I was so excited when I knew you were coming, and I so hoped that you would be a girl. During that time I began praying for your early salvation and for your mate in the years to come.

You arrived two weeks early, 5 lbs. & 9 oz., and how we praised the Lord for our healthy little daughter. You were 11 months old before you cut your 1st tooth and were still absolutely bald. I thought you were beautiful. I would rock you and hold you close and whisper in your little ear, "Jesus loves you, Jennie dear."

Early in life I saw the Holy Spirit working in you, and I had the privilege of seeing you invite the Lord Jesus into your heart at an early age. Do you remember how we rejoiced together that day?

Dad and I watched you grow into a beautiful young woman. You had a mind of your own, which caused us a few moments of anxiety, but you had a genuine heart for God that was such an encouragement to us. The Lord had gifted you in many ways, and we prayed you would use those gifts to bring honor to him.

Tomorrow you and Graydon will establish your own home. I'm afraid I miss you already, just thinking of the empty place you will leave behind. But I know how dearly you love each other. Your face shines whenever you talk about him. Someday, when you kiss your own daughter good-bye on her wedding day, you'll understand just what a mixture joy and sorrow can make.

I love you, Jennie, and I love the young man you have chosen. Tomorrow will be a day for rejoicing! I pray that together you will love God, trust him, serve him, and honor him. Love each other with all your heart, honey, but love your Savior even more. It's the real secret of happiness.

Love, Mother

Mary and Joseph discovered that very secret. It required that they let go of most of their own plans to let God have his way with their lives. In the end, they had to let go again, because the

Christ child Mary bore and the little boy they loved and raised wasn't really their child at all. He was their Savior.

A Whispered Prayer

Dear Heavenly Father, so often I forget that you want first place in my life. It's pretty scary, thinking of letting go of my own plans and allowing you to direct my life. Help me to trust you like Mary did, even when the path seems difficult. Help me to remember that with God nothing is impossible. Thank you for sending the Messiah! In the precious name of Jesus, Amen.

Get Up and Go Ideas for Tomorrow

1. I will take some time to examine the goals I have for my life.
2. I will surrender those plans to God, inviting his input, blessing, or redirection.

A Thought to Ponder as I Fall Asleep

Is my relationship with God more important to me than the opinion of others?

The Scripture Reading: Luke 1:1–4, 26–45, 56; 2:1–20

Many have undertaken to draw up an account of the things that have been fulfilled among us, just as they were handed down to us by those who from the first were eyewitnesses and servants of the word. Therefore, since I myself have carefully investigated everything from the beginning, it seemed good also to me to write an orderly account for you, most excellent Theophilus, so that you may know the certainty of the things you have been taught. . . .

In the sixth month, God sent the angel Gabriel to Nazareth, a town in Galilee, to a virgin pledged to be married to a man named Joseph, a descendant of David. The virgin's name was Mary. The angel went to her and said, "Greetings, you who are highly favored! The Lord is with you."

Mary was greatly troubled at his words and wondered what kind of greeting this might be. But the angel said to her, "Do not be afraid, Mary, you have found favor with God. You will be with child and give birth to a son, and you are to give him the name Jesus. He will be great and will be called the Son of the Most High. The Lord God will give him the throne of his father David, and he will reign over the house of Jacob forever; his kingdom will never end."

"How will this be," Mary asked the angel, "since I am a virgin?"

The angel answered, "The Holy Spirit will come upon you, and the power of the Most High will overshadow you. So the holy one to be born will be called the Son of God. Even Elizabeth your relative is going to have a child in her old age, and she who was said to be barren is in her sixth month. For nothing is impossible with God."

"I am the Lord's servant," Mary answered. "May it be to me as you have said." Then the angel left her.

At that time Mary got ready and hurried to a town in the hill country of Judea, where she entered Zechariah's home and greeted Elizabeth. When Elizabeth heard Mary's greeting, the baby leaped in her womb, and Elizabeth was filled with the Holy Spirit. In a loud voice she exclaimed: "Blessed are you among women, and blessed is the child you will bear! But why am I so favored, that the mother of my Lord should come to me? As soon as the sound of your greeting reached my ears, the baby in my womb leaped for joy. Blessed is she who has believed that what the Lord has said to her will be accomplished!" . . .

Mary stayed with Elizabeth for about three months and then returned home. . . .

In those days Caesar Augustus issued a decree that a census should be taken of the entire Roman world. (This was the first census that took place while Quirinius was governor of Syria.) And everyone went to his own town to register.

So Joseph also went up from the town of Nazareth in Galilee to Judea, to Bethlehem the town of David, because he belonged to the house and line of David. He went there to register with Mary, who was pledged to be married to him and was expecting a child. While they were there, the time came for the baby to be born, and she gave birth to her firstborn, a son. She wrapped him in cloths and placed him in a manger, because there was no room for them in the inn.

And there were shepherds living out in the fields nearby, keeping watch over their flocks at night. An angel of the Lord appeared to them, and the glory of the Lord shone around them, and they were terrified. But the angel said to them, "Do not be afraid. I bring you good news of great joy that will be for all the people. Today in the town of David a Savior has been born to you; he is Christ the Lord. This will be a sign to you: You will find a baby wrapped in cloths and lying in a manger."

Suddenly a great company of the heavenly host appeared with the angel, praising God and saying,

"Glory to God in the highest,
    and on earth peace to men on
        whom his favor rests."

When the angels had left them and gone into heaven, the shepherds said to one another, "Let's go to Bethlehem and see this thing that has happened, which the Lord has told us about."

So they hurried off and found Mary and Joseph, and the baby, who was lying in the manger. When they had seen him, they spread the word concerning what had been told them about this child, and all who heard it were amazed at what the shepherds said to them. But Mary treasured up all these things and pondered them in her heart. The shepherds returned, glorifying and praising God for all the things they had heard and seen, which were just as they had been told.

Final Note: Luke's carefully researched account of the nativity was recorded to prove the validity of Jesus Christ to non-Jewish readers. It was written in approximately AD 61–62.[8] The next chapter of *More Night Whispers* will point out other proofs that the Christ child was indeed the Messiah.

SEVEN

The Runaway Bride (and Groom and Baby)

A Story about Obedience, God's Protection, and a Family on the Run

My husband stood beside me, holding our ten-month-old daughter at the front of the church. Feeling a bit emotional, I blinked away a tear and tried to concentrate on what the minister was saying.

Amber Joy caught my eye in her white, lacy dress and tiny patent leather shoes. Her dark hair was arranged with a curl on top of her head, and she smelled like Baby Magic lotion. I loved her so much it almost hurt me to look at her.

Graydon and I were married nine years before we started our family, and that little girl was the answer to my prayers. What a gift from God she was to us! That morning we were dedicating our child—giving her back to God—but part of me wanted to snatch her away for fear he would allow something I did not want to happen in her life. However, the wiser part of me let go. Bottom line, I wanted God's will for my daughter's life, and the dedication service was our opportunity to say this publicly.

WHEN JESUS WAS BORN, Mary and Joseph were careful to observe the Jewish laws and customs that were required after the birth of a firstborn son. God honored their obedience with even more affirmation regarding who the baby really was, but there was danger afoot as well. As our story opens, Mary and Joseph are still in Bethlehem. Due to ceremonial requirements that would continue over several months, they had settled in the area.

Snapshots from the First Three Years

Mary looked around the simple room with a thankful heart as Joseph carried in their few belongings. With the city so crowded with people coming and going for the census, it was a miracle that Joseph had been able to find a place for them to stay. Looking down at the sleeping baby in her arms, she smiled and nodded. Miracle indeed. God had provided this place for them, just as he had provided the stable when she couldn't stay on the donkey another minute.

Joseph had been pleased with the lean-to that jutted out from the small house. "I'll make a sign and set up shop out there," he said optimistically. He glanced away from Mary to survey the

160

room, which offered only a lone, crudely made table. "Good thing you have a husband who loves to make benches," he said to her with a wink. Then, noting the lines of weariness on her face, he spread out a sleeping pallet. "You look so tired, Mary. You need to rest."

"Rest?" Mary said. "I need to clean this place and grind grain for bread. I need water to wash swaddling cloths, and I want to try to get the stains out of the blanket we used for the birthing—"

"And you need to rest, Mary. This is the time of your confinement, so try to enjoy it for at least an hour," he insisted, steering her to the pallet. "You know you're not allowed to be outside for another week, so I'll haul the water. I want you to sleep for now. The little one will have you up again before you know it."

MARY'S CONFINEMENT lasted for seven days. The eighth day was a cause for celebration and just a bit of anxiety for the new mother. On that day the Christ child was circumcised and given the name Jesus, as the angel Gabriel had instructed.

The days that followed were busy for the young family. Joseph had picked up several small carpentry jobs, and in between these he produced the bench he had promised. For Mary, laundry was a daily task now that the baby was with them, and she would either tie him on her back or carry him in a sling hung over her shoulder when she went to fetch the water. She also ground grain daily for their little household, rationing the supplies they had left.

Pausing a moment to feed more grain into the small grinder, she glanced at the peaceful infant napping on her pallet and then went back to working the stone to crush the hulls. Their meals were simple and rarely contained meat, but the olives, lentils, and occasional cheese she served with the bread were nourishing.

ABOUT A MONTH AFTER Jesus was circumcised, Mary and Joseph traveled from Bethlehem to Jerusalem to present Jesus at the temple.

"Oh, Joseph! Isn't it beautiful?" Mary said, stopping to gaze with wonder at the majesty of the temple up ahead. This was a special day for Mary—the day of her purification ceremony, exactly forty days after giving birth to a son, and the day they would present the infant, Jesus, to God. She had seen the temple at Jerusalem before, but the significance of the day and the fact that she would no longer be ceremonially unclean made her appreciate it anew.

"Yes, it is, Mary," her husband responded with a smile. "And I think it is a mysterious gift we bring to God this day," he added, reaching over to touch the downy softness of the baby's head. "We will offer to God his very own Son."

As Mary and Joseph crossed a large, open space within the temple walls, they were startled by the joyful cry of an old man who was hurrying toward them as fast as his feeble legs could carry him. He approached them with open arms. Mary and Joseph glanced at each other questioningly when they noticed the tears lining the man's wrinkled cheeks.

"Praise the sovereign Lord!" he wept, gazing at the baby in Mary's arms and holding out a trembling hand. "He has kept his promise to me!"

Strangely moved by the man's emotion, Mary looked at Joseph. When he nodded to her, she slowly uncovered the baby and held him out. The man, who introduced himself as Simeon, took the child in his arms, gently touching the baby's face with his gnarled, arthritic fingers.

Simeon laughed and then suddenly began to pray aloud. "You have kept your promise to me, Lord, and I am ready to die in peace. My eyes have seen your salvation, which you have prepared in the sight of all people, a light for revelation to the Gentiles and for glory to your people Israel."

He knows who Jesus is! Mary thought. *He knows Jesus is the Messiah!*

Then Simeon turned and blessed them, pausing to look long into Mary's eyes before he prophesied, his voice wavering with emotion.

"This child is destined to cause the falling and rising of many in Israel, and many will speak against him. The thoughts of many hearts will be revealed." Then, pausing a moment, he looked again at Mary and added sadly, "And a sword will pierce your own soul too."

Mary inhaled sharply, and she felt Joseph's hand tighten on her arm. *People will speak against the Messiah?* she thought in confusion. *How can that be? A sword will pierce my soul?* For a moment she wanted to snatch Jesus away from the old man, but deep down she realized he was telling her the truth.

Just then, another cry of joy arrested their attention. Mary turned to see an elderly woman approaching them. "Praise be to the Lord God!" the woman cried. The woman introduced herself as Anna, and told them she had been a widow for many years and now spent all of her time praying and fasting at the temple. At the sight of the Christ child, she couldn't help but welcome him and his parents.

That night, Mary and Joseph marveled at all that had happened. At the day's beginning they had carefully planned to do everything required by the law of the Lord. By the day's end, they lifted joyful hearts to God for affirming again and again his own Son.

LOOKING UP FROM HER MENDING, Mary watched Jesus happily topple the short tower of wooden blocks he had managed to stack. *He's a fine, sturdy toddler,* she thought with a smile. Time had passed, and life had settled into a kind of normalcy, so Mary was surprised when Joseph opened the door and announced that they had special guests.

Mary stepped outside to greet their guests. *Special indeed!* she thought, startled to see several men dressed in rich robes standing in front of their humble dwelling. *They are strangers to this land,* she realized. At first glance she could see that one had skin of a darker tone than their own, and another had almond-shaped eyes and a kind smile.

Who are we to receive guests such as these? she wondered as she looked at their colorful robes and impressive headpieces. Turning to Joseph, who had sawdust smeared on one cheek and fine wood shavings stuck to an arm, she raised her eyebrows.

"They are Magi, wise men who have come far from the East to see Jesus, Mary," Joseph said. She could read excitement and a little nervousness in his voice. "They tell me they have followed a star to find the newborn king of the Jews, and they have come to worship him!"

A smile of welcome warmed Mary's face, and she gestured for the esteemed visitors to enter their home.

What a sight they were—royal guests kneeling on the floor, worshiping a little boy. Their joy at seeing the child was so genuine that Mary and Joseph's nervousness soon turned to wonder as they watched the men with little Jesus. These men were not Jewish, and yet they worshiped the Messiah! First they bowed low before him, and the child, fascinated by these men who were down on ground level with him, stared solemnly at them for a moment before gurgling gleefully and waving his chubby arms. The men laughed aloud and then presented gifts of great value, the like of which Mary and Joseph had never seen before. Gold, incense, and myrrh.

There weren't enough benches for the men to sit down, even after Joseph carried in a wooden crate from his workshop, but it didn't seem to matter to their wealthy guests. As evening approached and they shared a humble supper with the little family, the wise men from the East told the story of how they had come to find the child.

"We stopped first in Jerusalem," they said, "to inquire of King Herod where the royal child was."

Joseph stiffened at this news. Mary looked at him in worry. Herod was protective of his title of king to the point of paranoia.

"He seemed most excited," they said, "and called his own wise men together to determine where the child was predicted to be born. After some study, they reported to him that the place of birth was Bethlehem. Herod then came to us privately and questioned us as to the exact time we had first seen the star. He instructed us to find the babe and to report back to him so that he too could come and worship the child." The speaker was sitting cross-legged on the floor and smiled across the room at Mary, who was also sitting on the floor with the babe asleep in her lap. "We have longed to find and worship him for almost two years," the wise man said with emotion. "Today is the fulfillment of our mission."

Their guests retired for the night, sleeping outside under the starry sky that had led them to the Christ child. But their sleep was troubled. Warned in a dream that they should not go back to their own country by way of Jerusalem, they said their warm good-byes the next morning and departed for their homeland, taking an alternate route.

"MARY! MARY, WAKE UP," Joseph whispered the following evening, shaking her shoulder until she stirred into wakefulness.

Alarmed, she immediately reached out to feel the baby sleeping peacefully nearby her. "What is it, Joseph? What's the matter?"

"We must leave now, Mary! Gather a few things quickly and leave the rest. Pack the gifts from the Magi, some food, and what you must have for the baby. I'll bring the donkey around. God has warned me in a dream that Herod means to harm Jesus. He told me to take you and the baby to Egypt and to wait there until he tells me otherwise, because Herod is going to search for the child to kill him. We'll talk later, but for now, work as fast as you can!"

Mary sprang into action, her heart pounding with fear and dismay.

THEY SLIPPED AWAY in the middle of the night, headed for a foreign land. As Joseph urged the little donkey along the dark road, Mary found herself clutching the warm little body nestled against her. Leaving in such a manner reminded her of the night they had arrived in Bethlehem and how God had provided for them. Her racing heartbeat steadied, and she relaxed her grip on the baby with a sigh. God would take care of them.

They traveled for many days, from Bethlehem in the high country to the lowlands. When they finally reached Gaza, the last major town before facing the desert, Joseph traded some of the gold from the Magi for supplies and purchased extra goatskins for water and a small tent to protect them from the blowing sand at night. As the desert stretched out before them, they thought of their forefathers who had long ago sought refuge in the land of Egypt. Mary and Joseph had been born and raised in the small village of Nazareth—their travel had been limited to pilgrimages back and forth from Jerusalem for religious purposes. The impromptu world travelers were as unprepared for the sights and sounds that would confront them in Egypt as their forefather Joseph had been.

"How strange to be fleeing for safety to the land where our people were once held captive," Mary whispered to Joseph as they camped one night along the way. She had nursed the baby, and he was sleeping soundly between them.

"It's probably the last place Herod would think to look," Joseph said with a yawn. "Let's get some sleep, Mary. Tomorrow we should reach the Nile."

HEROD PACED IMPATIENTLY back and forth in his bedchamber, his mind working furiously over the matter of the Magi who had come seeking the child destined to be King of the Jews. *They should have been back two days ago!* he thought in exasperation, and then his frustration turned to fury.

Those scheming foreigners have tricked me! he realized. "They have outwitted me!" he growled aloud in a burst of anger. "Guards!" he shouted. "Come immediately!"

Grief raged in Bethlehem as a military contingent under Herod's command invaded the village, killing every male child under the age of two.

GREAT PYRAMIDS ROSE UP in the distance as the little family approached Egypt. The language, the architecture, the food, the pagan worship—everything was foreign to them, but they were *safe*. Far from the wrath of King Herod, they settled as aliens in the land of Egypt. How grateful they were for the gifts from the Magi, which enabled them to secure food, shelter, and supplies.

Time passed, and loneliness occasionally overwhelmed Mary, leaving her longing for the familiarity of home. Then she would recall the faithfulness of God and the many affirmations of his mighty hand on their lives, and peace would come. "With God, nothing is impossible," she would whisper. "Nothing is impossible with God."

ONE MORNING, just as dawn was breaking, Mary awoke to find Joseph lying beside her wide awake, studying her face in the semidarkness. "Is everything all right?" she whispered.

He grinned broadly. "Oh yes, dear Mary," he said, reaching out to capture her chin between his thumb and forefinger. "Would you like to go home?"

Mary sat up. "Are you teasing me, Joseph? Please say you're not!"

Joseph gathered her into his arms as he explained. "The Lord came to me in a dream again last night. He told me that Herod is dead and that it is safe to go back to the land of Israel."

This time, packing was a joy and the trip an adventure, with little Jesus often riding on Joseph's shoulders, his small voice calling out in excitement as he pointed at one thing or another along the way.

When they finally arrived in the land of Israel, Joseph learned that Herod's son, Archelaus, was reigning as king of Judah in his father's place. Rather than move back to Bethlehem, which was near Jerusalem and Herod's son, Joseph moved his little family to Nazareth in the district of Galilee, which was about ninety miles farther north. They were finally home.

There the child grew strong; he was filled with wisdom, and the grace of God was upon him.

Digging Deeper

Jesus was born during a period in history when the entire Mediterranean world was dominated by the powerful Roman Empire. "Its science, philosophy, theology, wealth . . . and social power reigned supreme and were in opposition to any such idea as the coming of a Messiah."[1] In the midst of this opposition we have Mary, Joseph, and the Christ child entering the scene.

What affirmation did God give Mary and Joseph? In asking them to carry out his incredible plan, God did not leave them wandering in the dark. I reviewed their story and came up with an incredible list of "affirming moments." Here are just some of them: (1) Gabriel's visit to Mary; (2) Elizabeth's miracle pregnancy and Gabriel's visit with Zechariah; (3) Elizabeth's announcement that Mary was "the mother of my Lord"; (4) God speaking to Joseph in a dream; (5) angel voices heralding the Savior's birth; (6) the shepherds worshiping the Christ child; (7) old Simeon at the temple, recognizing Jesus as the promised Messiah; (8) Anna the widow at the temple, testifying; (9) the amazing visit of the wise men, and God's warning for them to go home another way; (10) God's warning to Joseph to flee from Herod into Egypt; and (11) God informing Joseph in a dream when it was safe to return home.

Wow! Their assignment wasn't easy, but there were plenty of affirming memories for Mary to "treasure" in her heart and to give Joseph confidence along the way.

What religious ceremonies did Mary and Joseph observe following Jesus' birth? Following the birth of a male child, the mother was to stay confined at home for seven days (fourteen days if she bore a daughter). Circumcision and naming were first on the list for Jewish baby boys, and this ceremony occurred on the eighth day after birth. Who circumcised Jesus? Maybe Joseph. Bible culture expert Ralph Gower gives some very interesting insight: "The male baby was circumcised either by the head of the family or by a physician. . . . The naming of the child frequently accompanied the act of circumcision. This happened in Jesus' case (Luke 2:21)."[2]

Following the naming and circumcision ceremony was ritual purification for the mother, which was required by Old Testament law. (You can read about it in Leviticus 12:1–8.) After the birth of a male child, the mother was considered unclean for forty days—eighty days for a girl! After that time, she was to go to the temple and offer a lamb with a pigeon or dove as a sin offering to restore her fellowship with God. Remember, in Old Testament times a woman's menstrual cycle rendered her ceremonially unclean, and the bleeding following childbirth did the same thing. Gower points out a practical side to these rules, as "it was a means of protecting a woman from sexual relations in times of weakness,"[3] although why she should need longer to heal after having a daughter confounds me!

If the family were poor, they could substitute another dove for the lamb, which is what Mary and Joseph did. That should give us a hint regarding how humbly they lived during the early days of Jesus' life.

Who were Simeon and Anna? Simeon was an elderly, devout Jew who was filled with the spirit of God. He longed for the redemption of Israel, and it had been revealed to him that he would see the Savior before he died. He was moved by the Spirit of God to go to the temple the day Mary and Joseph brought Jesus for dedication.

Anna was an elderly prophetess from the tribe of Asher. Anna had been widowed after being married for only seven years, and the Scripture says she never left the temple grounds, where she worshiped God day and night, fasting and praying. A respected woman, her thanksgiving to God for the child and the fact that she reported his birth to "all who were looking forward to the redemption of Jerusalem" (Luke 2:38) must have been another great affirmation for Mary and Joseph.

Who were the wise men? Not mentioned by Luke but reported by Matthew, these men did not come to the stable like our nativity scenes portray, but came later to a home in Bethlehem where Joseph and Mary went to stay after Jesus was born. Commentator Walter Elwell tells us that the Magi or "wise men" from the East probably traveled from Babylon. The exact number of esteemed visitors is not known, but those that came "honored Jesus as King—as one already a king and not merely destined to become one."[4] Elwell goes on to explain:

> The Magi's visit is prompted by a star, variously identified as a comet, a supernova, a planetary conjunction, or a unique supernatural phenomenon. The Magi's language ("his star," v. 2) strongly suggests that they . . . studied the Scriptures as well as the heavens. Was not a star to herald Israel's king?[5]

How serious a threat was Herod? A very serious threat. Called Herod the Great, he was charming enough to be friends with Mark Antony and other famed Roman rulers, and merciless enough to have several of his own sons put to death.[6]

I found it interesting to learn that

> one of Herod's greatest problems was that Cleopatra, now married to Mark Antony, wanted to bring Palestine back under the control of Egypt. Fortunately for Herod, Antony was neither willing nor able to agree to such a course of action. But he did

give some chunks of Herod's domain to Cleopatra . . . [who] continued to give him grief.[7]

Dependent on the Roman government for his position as king, Herod played both sides from the middle. He kept Rome happy by taxing the Jews, building impressive structures and naming them for his Roman friends, and providing military assistance to Rome when needed. However, he had to be careful not to push his subjects, the Jews, too far for fear of rebellion, which would cause Rome to question his ability to rule.

Herod the Great was an amazing builder, responsible for rebuilding the temple in Jerusalem, but he was ruthless and so paranoid about losing his throne that he ordered all the Jewish boy babies under age two murdered in an attempt to kill the infant Jesus. Herod died when Jesus was still quite young and living in exile.

It is interesting to note that the visit of the Magi provided gifts that very likely helped to support the little family on their long journey as they fled from Herod into the land of Egypt.

Did Mary and Joseph have a real marriage? According to Matthew 13:55 and John 7:3–5, Mary and Joseph had other children besides Jesus. Those named in Scripture are James, Joseph, Simon, and Judas, plus an unspecified number of sisters (Matt. 13:55–56). We are not told when they were born but only that his brothers doubted that Jesus was the Messiah until he rose from the grave. After Christ's ascension into heaven, his brothers became key leaders in the early Christian church movement. James and Judas (Jude) each authored a book in the New Testament.

The last mention of Joseph, the husband of Mary, in Scripture was when twelve-year-old Jesus stayed behind at the temple and his parents had to come looking for him. Young Jewish boys celebrated manhood at age thirteen, and scholars agree that it is likely that Joseph died before Jesus began his public ministry at age thirty. I smile thinking of Joseph arriving in heaven and hearing God say, "Welcome home, Joseph. Well done! You have been a good and faithful servant."

How can you apply this story to your life?

Remember that nothing is impossible with God. Mary and Joseph faced challenges that must have seemed overwhelming at times. When God asks you to do something that you think is too difficult, remember that when we surrender our will to his, he will affirm that he is with us all along the way.

Consider parenting as a gift and a sacred charge. God gave Mary a miracle baby and charged both Mary and Joseph with the responsibility of raising him to maturity. If you are a parent, do you consider your children a gift from God, and the job of raising them a sacred responsibility? Have you acknowledged that your children are not really yours but God's? Are you teaching your children to know God and to walk in his ways?

Decide to help a family in need. I've never been politically oppressed and had to run for my life, but many people in the world have done just that to protect their own lives or the lives of their children.

After studying Mary and Joseph's escape into Egypt with the infant Jesus, I went online to research modern-day refugees. The number of persecuted people longing for freedom is staggering. They hail from Bosnia, Somalia, Afghanistan, China, Vietnam, Chile, and Sri Lanka, to name just a few. The story of the "Lost Boys" from Sudan was particularly wrenching but has a happy ending because of Christians willing to reach out. Mission and social agencies are begging for help, and you and your church can make a difference—not just in this lifetime but for eternity.

There may be lonely individuals or families in your own community who have come to this country to establish a new life. Ask God if this is an area where he could use you, and then put feet to your resolve as you befriend and share his love with others. When you feel inadequate to the task, remember that nothing is impossible with God.

I SAT IN THE FRONT ROW spellbound as I listened to the woman's story of tragedy, healing, desire for freedom, and daring escape. I was speaking for a large Women Alive conference in Waterloo, Ontario, and Kim Phuc had been invited to speak as well. I had been anxious to hear her story; I remembered seeing her picture when I was a young teenager during the Vietnam War. Kim Phuc was the naked, chemically burned child who was captured on film as she ran from a napalm bomb attack on her village. It was one of the most haunting images of the war.

After the bombing, Kim had to live through a long and excruciating healing process that included many painful surgeries and treatments. In the meantime, her picture was being shown around the world, and the Viet Cong decided to use her as a propaganda tool against the United States. In addition to learning to survive the pain and disfigurement that resulted from the severe burns, Kim was put on display, photographed, and made to speak about her ordeal. Considered valuable to the government, she was guarded constantly, even while she slept. This persecution went on for years.

That day as I listened, Kim told of her great unhappiness and longing for love and freedom. She told of how she had come to know Jesus, and the joy that he brought into her life. She shared how she met her husband, who also was a Christian, and finally how they had escaped from the guards while on their honeymoon, with only her purse and the clothes on their backs. Like Mary and Joseph of old, they ran for their lives. Fear of the unknown and loneliness followed, but they were free.

Today Kim speaks around the world on the subjects of peace and forgiveness. She was an honored guest at the dedication of the Vietnam Memorial, and she and her husband are now Canadian citizens. They have two young sons, and Kim's parents recently defected from Vietnam and are also living safely in Canada.

A Whispered Prayer

Dear Heavenly Father, give me an obedient heart like Joseph, Lord, and help me to be sensitive to your direction in my life as a parent and as your representative to others. My life is so easy compared with those of people who have no personal freedom or who struggle just to survive. Thank you for the many ways you have blessed me, and please show me how you want me to help others. In the precious name of Jesus, Amen.

Get Up and Go Ideas for Tomorrow

1. I will bring a plate of cookies or a loaf of bread to a new family in my community.

175

2. I will follow up with inviting them into my home and then inviting them to church.

A Thought to Ponder as I Fall Asleep

How would I react if a family of another race moved next door to me? Would I shun or welcome them?

The Scripture Reading: Luke 2:21–40; Matthew 2:1–23

On the eighth day, when it was time to circumcise him, he was named Jesus, the name the angel had given him before he had been conceived.

When the time of their purification according to the Law of Moses had been completed, Joseph and Mary took him to Jerusalem to present him to the Lord (as it is written in the Law of the Lord, "Every firstborn male is to be consecrated to the Lord"), and to offer a sacrifice in keeping with what is said in the Law of the Lord: "a pair of doves or two young pigeons."

Now there was a man in Jerusalem called Simeon, who was righteous and devout. He was waiting for the consolation of Israel, and the Holy Spirit was upon him. It had been revealed to him by the Holy Spirit that he would not die before he had seen the Lord's Christ. Moved by the Spirit, he went into the temple courts. When the parents brought in the child Jesus to do for him what the custom of the Law required, Simeon took him in his arms and praised God, saying:

"Sovereign Lord, as you have promised, you now dismiss your servant in peace.

For my eyes have seen your salvation,
  which you have prepared in the
  sight of all people,
a light for revelation to the Gentiles
  and for glory to your people
  Israel."

The child's father and mother marveled at what was said about him. Then Simeon blessed them and said to Mary, his mother: "This child is destined to cause the falling and rising of many in Israel, and to be a sign that will be spoken against, so that the thoughts of many hearts will be revealed. And a sword will pierce your own soul too."

There was also a prophetess, Anna, the daughter of Phanuel, of the tribe of Asher. She was very old; she had lived with her husband seven years after her marriage, and then was a widow until she was eighty-four. She never left the temple but worshiped night and day, fasting and praying. Coming up to them at that very moment, she gave thanks to God and spoke about the child to all who were looking forward to the redemption of Jerusalem.

When Joseph and Mary had done everything required by the Law of the Lord, they returned to Galilee to their own town of Nazareth. And the child grew and became strong; he was filled with wisdom, and the grace of God was upon him. . . .

After Jesus was born in Bethlehem in Judea, during the time of King Herod, Magi from the east came to Jerusalem and asked, "Where is the one who has been born king of the Jews? We saw his star in the east and have come to worship him."

When King Herod heard this he was disturbed, and all Jerusalem with him. When he had called together all the people's chief priests and teachers of the law, he asked them where the Christ was to be born. "In Bethlehem in Judea," they replied, "for this is what the prophet has written:

"'But you, Bethlehem, in the land of
      Judah,
   are by no means least among the
      rulers of Judah;
for out of you will come a ruler
   who will be the shepherd of my
      people Israel.'"

Then Herod called the Magi secretly and found out from them the exact time the star had appeared. He sent them to Bethlehem and said, "Go and make a careful search for the child. As soon as you find him, report to me, so that I too may go and worship him."

After they had heard the king, they went on their way, and the star they had seen in the east went ahead of them until it stopped over the place where the child was. When they saw the star, they were overjoyed. On coming to the house, they saw the child with

his mother Mary, and they bowed down and worshiped him. Then they opened their treasures and presented him with gifts of gold and of incense and of myrrh. And having been warned in a dream not to go back to Herod, they returned to their country by another route.

When they had gone, an angel of the Lord appeared to Joseph in a dream. "Get up," he said, "take the child and his mother and escape to Egypt. Stay there until I tell you, for Herod is going to search for the child to kill him."

So he got up, took the child and his mother during the night and left for Egypt, where he stayed until the death of Herod. And so was fulfilled what the Lord had said through the prophet: "Out of Egypt I called my son."

When Herod realized that he had been outwitted by the Magi, he was furious, and he gave orders to kill all the boys in Bethlehem and its vicinity who were two years old and under, in accordance with the time he had learned from the Magi. Then what was said through the prophet Jeremiah was fulfilled:

"A voice is heard in Ramah,
   weeping and great mourning,
Rachel weeping for her children
   and refusing to be comforted,
because they are no more."

After Herod died, an angel of the Lord appeared in a dream to Joseph in Egypt and said, "Get up, take the child and his mother and go to the land of Israel, for those who were trying to take the child's life are dead."

So he got up, took the child and his mother and went to the land of Israel. But when he heard that Archelaus was reigning in Judea in place of his father Herod, he was afraid to go there. Having been warned in a dream, he withdrew to the district of Galilee, and he went and lived in a town called Nazareth. So was fulfilled what was said through the prophets: "He will be called a Nazarene."

Final Note: The Gospel of Matthew was written for Jews and carefully gave Old Testament references throughout to prove that Jesus was the long expected Messiah. Matthew "collected Jesus' sermons and stories. He preserved them in a book that some call a new Torah because Jesus fulfilled so much Old Testament prophecy and restated much of the Mosaic Law."[8]

The Untouchables

Two Stories about God's
Healing Touch

The photos were grossly riveting. I had been casually leafing backward through the *National Geographic* magazine on my lap when a photo of two women scavenging through a pile of chicken bones in the garbage caught my eye. Other photos showed women breathing thick, red dust as they loaded thousands of rusty colored bricks onto carts and doing hard labor in a rock quarry. The word *untouchables* leaped out from the page. The entire headline read: "Branded as impure from the moment of birth, one out of six Indians lives—and suffers—at the bottom of the Hindu caste system. They are UNTOUCHABLES."[1]

The article went on to explain that if people, and there are 160 million of them, are born into this lower social order, they are doomed to be rejected by the rest of Hindu society. Their crime is simply being born. "Untouchables are outcasts—people considered too impure, too polluted to rank as worthy beings. Prejudice defines their lives. . . . Untouchables are shunned, insulted, banned from temples . . . made to eat and drink from separate utensils in public places" and made to perform the most menial and disgusting jobs.[2] Their touch is considered unclean. In some areas they are even required to live downwind from upper classes so that others are not forced to breathe their air.

Each paragraph I read saddened me more than the last.

I was particularly interested in the article because just the week before, I had received an invitation to go to India with my friend Barb Potter for Mission India, a literacy program for women. As I stared at the pages of the magazine that day, the great need Barb had described to me became a graphic reality. It also reminded me of two socially "untouchable" females in Scripture who experienced new lives because of Jesus—who hadn't found them untouchable at all.

Two Miracles

The woman paused from her labor with a weary sigh. Beneath her head covering she looked older than her years, with her pale, drawn face and thin hair. Bending again to her task, she dipped blood-stained rags into the cool water and scrubbed them vigorously against a rock.

Several women were crouched at the shoreline, doing laundry on the northwestern shore of the Sea of Galilee. Fishing boats dotted the seascape before them, and hills rose up behind them and around the bustling city of Capernaum.

An older woman approached with her own basket of garments and paused for a moment. "How long have you been bleeding, girl?"

Startled by the bold inquiry, the younger woman glanced up. She didn't intend to answer such a question, but her gaze was arrested for a moment by the mixture of kindness and pity she read on the wrinkled face gazing down at her. She didn't often encounter such an expression in a community that avoided her.

"Twelve years," she said simply, going back to her scrubbing. "It never stops."

The old woman stepped closer. "Surely there's a cure."

"No, I've spent all I have going from physician to physician." She slapped a rag against the rock and looked up. "I've tried every treatment, and believe me, some of those so-called cures weren't very pleasant." Emotion swept over her; embarrassed, she looked away from the woman and stared out at the sea. "I'm afraid that rather than help me, those cures only made my condition worse."

THE OLD WOMAN could read volumes in the words of the pale creature bending in the gentle waves. She imagined the loneliness of never being allowed in the synagogue, of never being touched intimately by a husband; she imagined the abuse by so-called doctors; she imagined being judged unclean and being helpless to do a thing about it.

"I think you should go to Jesus," the old woman stated simply. "He can make you well."

"Oh, I wouldn't dare," the younger woman responded, shaking her head. "I try to avoid crowds so as not to offend anyone with my presence. There are always so many people around him. And besides, my condition is too shameful to speak about publicly."

181

The elderly woman set down her basket of garments. "Think about it, little one. Jesus heals the sick and changes the lives of those who believe in him."

"I've heard that he and his men have left the area." The younger woman's voice was filled with longing.

"Oh, Jesus will be back," the old woman assured her. She gestured to some fishing vessels in the distance. "This is where he called his first disciples to leave their nets and follow him, and he teaches often in the synagogue here. He'll be back."

THE MAN CLOSED HIS EYES and swallowed hard, a wave of misery sweeping over him as he stood in the doorway of the sickroom. His daughter lay motionless on the narrow bed, her delicate face deathly white and her breathing shallow. His wife sat beside her, weeping quietly, and he knew that hired mourners and well-meaning neighbors were already gathering in preparation for the funeral.

Helplessness overwhelmed him. He had paid for the best physicians, but it was all for nothing. He was in a position of influence, but in this situation, he was powerless.

If only . . . A sigh of frustration escaped as he thought again of Jesus. As ruler of the synagogue, Jairus had watched and listened when the controversial rabbi had taught there in Capernaum, and as an elder, he had heard the joyful testimonies of some who had been healed. But he had also listened to the heated criticism by other religious leaders and had chosen to stay out of the fray.

As time went by, however, Jairus's own heart had been stirred by the rabbi's message. Still, he had not dared to seek Jesus out—until it was too late. Jesus had left with his disciples by boat, and Jairus could do nothing but watch helplessly as his daughter's condition worsened.

He was startled out of his reverie by a faithful servant who had just arrived at the house.

"Master, he is back!" his servant stated breathlessly.

"What do you mean, man?" Jairus asked. "Who is back?"

"The teacher—Jesus! He has just arrived with his disciples by boat, and people are crowding around him. Come quickly, Master!"

Jairus left the house immediately, in search of Jesus.

AFTER CROSSING THE SEA of Galilee once again, Jesus and his disciples arrived in Capernaum. While they were still at the shore, people swarmed around them, eager to hear what Jesus had to say and to watch as he interacted with individuals who came to him. Jesus spoke to the crowd while his disciples gathered their few belongings.

Suddenly, a desperate voice arrested Jesus' attention as the crowd parted for Jairus, the ruler of the synagogue.

Jairus fell down at Jesus' feet and breathlessly begged for help. "Master, my little daughter is dying! I beg you to please come to my home and put your hands on her so that she will be healed and live!"

Reading both desperation and faith on the man's face, Jesus left immediately to follow Jairus to his home. But the curious crowd was so thick that Jesus and his disciples were pressed on all sides, and it was difficult to make their way through the streets.

ANOTHER DESPERATE PERSON was in the streets that day. The hemorrhaging woman had been watching the crowd come together from a distance, her heart pounding furiously as she gathered her courage to approach Jesus.

He's my last hope, she thought to herself, taking a step forward and then hesitating a moment. She pulled her head covering lower over her face, for fear she might be recognized as an un-touchable, and took a few more steps. She lost sight of Jesus for a moment, so she craned her neck to see. It looked like Jesus was changing directions.

Her mind was working overtime as she hurried to catch up to him. *I can't interrupt him. No, I won't bother him, but if I could just touch the hem of his garment, I'll be healed.* She forced her feet to move into the crowd and then ducked and pressed her way closer to Jesus. She was terrified, but despite her fear, a hope that she hadn't felt for years filled her heart. More than hope, there was simple faith that Jesus had the power to change her life. *Perhaps he won't be angry if I simply touch the fringe on his robe . . .*

She was close now, and in her intensity, she forgot the jos-tling crowd. Jesus was just ahead, and in the next instant, she managed to reach between the men ahead of her and brush her hand against the fringe of his garment.

SHE STOOD STOCK STILL as healing washed over her. Strength flowed through her veins, and joy flooded her soul as she rec-ognized that she had been cleansed of her sickness. The crowd pressed on, but she was so overwhelmed with what had happened that she simply stood where she was.

Suddenly Jesus stopped. "Who touched me?"

One of his disciples gave him an incredulous look. "Master, you're surrounded by a multitude and have been bumped by at least a hundred people in this street. Now you're asking who touched you?"

The woman stood frozen as she waited for the Master's eyes to meet hers. *He knows it was me. I had no right to touch him. I was bleeding, and now my touch has made him ritually unclean.*

She had never been more frightened in her life. And yet, she had never been more joyful. Jesus had healed her. Her grateful heart exploded with thanksgiving.

Throwing herself at his feet, she confessed everything. The bleeding, the doctors, her despair, and most of all her faith in Jesus, the one who had made her whole again.

While pious men stepped away from her, Jesus did not. "Daughter," he said warmly, "your faith has healed you. You can leave here in peace, knowing that you are free from your suffering."

THE CROWD WAS CAUGHT UP in the drama that was taking place between Jesus and the woman who had been unclean. Even Jairus was moved by the miracle, but he knew the delay it caused was critical to his own mission. As he turned to urge the disciples to hurry Jesus along, Jairus was interrupted by messengers from home.

"Jairus! We're sorry, but your daughter is dead," the men told him solemnly. "Come back to mourn with the others, and do not trouble the teacher anymore."

Jairus turned to Jesus with a look of despair, but Jesus locked eyes with him and said, "Don't be afraid; just believe." And suddenly, the despair faded away from Jairus, and his heart was filled with quiet trust. Then Jesus dismissed the crowd, allowing only three of his disciples, Peter, James, and John, to go on with him to Jairus's home.

THE NOISE WAS DEAFENING. Stepping over the threshold into the wealthy man's home, Jesus and his disciples were met with a chaotic example of what money could buy when it came to funerals. One level of noise layered another. Flute players were playing mournful tunes while paid mourners recited a mixture of tributes and dirges. Women with ashes on their heads wept loudly and beat their chests in anguish.

"What is all this commotion and wailing about?" Jesus asked, raising his voice above the din. "The child isn't dead, but sleeping."

When the crowd refuted his announcement with jeers and scornful laughter, Jesus had them all put out of the house. Then, in the quiet that followed, he led the child's parents and the three disciples into the room where the body lay.

Jairus and his wife watched in amazement as Jesus approached the girl and reached down to hold her hand. Then he spoke directly to her. "Little girl, I say to you, get up!"

Immediately the girl got up and started walking around the room. Her parents were dumbfounded. As they gathered their daughter in their arms and wept for joy, Jesus instructed them to give her something nourishing to eat.

Later, as the small group rejoiced together, Jesus told them firmly not to broadcast what had happened. People would know soon enough about the child as she resumed her normal life. As for Jairus, the ruler of the synagogue, he learned that proclaiming faith in Jesus Christ and trusting God's timing were well worth the risk.

Digging Deeper

At age thirty Jesus began his public ministry, which included turning water into wine at a wedding, teaching thousands of people who clamored around him, healing the sick, freeing the oppressed from demonic control, and calming storms, to list just a portion of his earthly activities. During that time he also mentored a core group of disciples who would carry on his work after his death, resurrection, and ascension into heaven. Scholars place the two miraculous incidents retold above in Capernaum, a city by the sea. It is interesting to note that "on and around the Sea of Galilee Jesus performed 18 of his 33 recorded miracles and issued most of His teachings to His disciples and the multitudes that followed Him."[3]

Although the Gospel writers, Matthew, Mark, Luke, and John, recorded only some of the miracles Jesus performed during those three years, three of them, Matthew, Mark, and Luke, recorded an account of the two miracles discussed in this chapter of *More Night Whispers*.

As I studied the two events, I found it helpful to understand the rules of the day regarding why the woman and the girl were considered untouchable, and to learn about Eastern customs for mourning a death. It was also helpful to imagine another female character with whom the bleeding woman might have spoken. Take a closer look at the stories with me.

Who were the risk takers in this story? Driven by desperate circumstances, both Jairus, the ruler of the local synagogue, and the hemorrhaging woman dared to come out in public to seek help from Jesus.

The Scripture tells us that Jairus approached Jesus in the middle of a pressing crowd of people and *begged* Jesus to come home with him and heal his twelve-year-old daughter, who at that moment was sick unto death. Jesus was a very controversial rabbi, and Jairus was employed by the Jewish religious system. He "was one of the rulers of the synagogue, which identifies him as one of the elders who were in charge of the services in the synagogue attended by Jesus at Capernaum."[4] A note in the Word in Life Study Bible explains the risk he took:

Jairus (Mark 5:22) risked his job as the ruler of the synagogue by turning to Jesus. This leader was well known in his town, and his actions were carefully watched by people.

But he was desperate to save his daughter's life. . . .

Some Jews followed [Jesus], but many others took great offense at His teaching (Mark 3:6). So when Jairus fell at Jesus' feet, he must have known that some in his synagogue would sharply criticize him.[5]

Jesus rewarded Jairus's faith by immediately turning to go with the ruler to his home, but he very likely tested Jairus's patience by pausing to deal with another risk taker along the way. It was significant to me that Jesus made an "important" man wait while he took time with someone most of the people would have judged as "unimportant."

Who was this woman? Well, she was considered "unclean" and had lived with that stigma for twelve long years. Because of a chronic bleeding condition, she was in ritual "confinement"—not for forty days, like the new mother of a baby boy, but every day. She knew not only the loss of health and strength but the loss of community and public worship. If she was married, her husband wouldn't want to touch her, lest he also be contaminated. A husband even could have used her condition as grounds for divorce. And she couldn't go to church, or in her case the temple or synagogue, because she was unclean. The woman had gone to many physicians in the hope of being cured, and at their hands suffered under some drastic forms of treatment that not only drained her of all her money but also left her in an even worse condition. A commentary note explains her situation more fully.

Jews considered women ritually unclean during menstruation, and whoever touched a menstruating woman was made unclean until evening. If a woman experienced bleeding other than her normal menses, she was considered unclean until the bleeding stopped (Lev. 15:19–27). That meant exclusion from participating in the life and worship of the community.

Scripture is silent on the source of this woman's livelihood. Perhaps she lived off an inheritance, or perhaps she was divorced and her dowry had been returned to her. Whatever her means of support, it was gone. Jesus was her last hope.[6]

By mixing with the pressing crowd and then daring to reach out to touch Jesus, she broke the rules, big time.

Why did Jesus ask who had touched him? Think about it. He was being rushed away by Jairus on an urgent mission, and the crowd was so thick that he and his disciples were being jostled around.

I believe Jesus knew exactly who had touched him and why, but that he drew the woman out for her own spiritual growth (and also to later increase Jairus's own faith). I appreciated William MacDonald's comment in the *Believer's Bible Commentary*:

Her plan was to slip away quietly, but the Lord would not let her miss the blessing of publicly acknowledging her Savior. His disciples thought the question was silly. . . . "Who touched me?" But there is a difference between the touch of physical nearness, and the touch of desperate faith. . . . She fell down before Him and made her first public confession of Jesus. . . . Open confession of Christ is of tremendous importance. Without it there can be little growth in the Christian life.[7]

Did Jesus recoil when the woman touched him and he realized that supernatural power had gone out of him? No. Technically, her touch would have rendered Jesus unclean, but rather than shun her, he stopped and asked for her public testimony (which must have terrified her, for fear he would be angry). He took time to encourage her, honored her for her faith, and sent her away healed and at peace for the first time in twelve years. His public affirmation in front of many witnesses and calling her by the endearing name of "Daughter" must have been an added balm to her wounded spirit, especially after being shunned publicly for over a decade. How like Jesus to minister to her every need—physically, spiritually, and emotionally.

Who was the other untouchable in this story? Jairus's deceased twelve-year-old daughter. While Jesus was healing the hemorrhaging woman, news came that the girl had died. Jesus' delay seemed fatal, but Jesus told Jairus, "Do not be afraid, only believe."

A corpse was considered unclean, and women were given the job of preparing bodies for burial, which often took place the same day as the death and always by the second day, due to the rapid decomposition of bodies in a hot climate. The classical commentator Matthew Henry explained how Jesus broke the rules and touched an untouchable once again.

> Christ went in and took her by the hand. . . . The high priest, that typified Christ, was not to come near the dead (Lev. xxi. 10, 11), but Christ *touched* the dead. The Levitical priesthood leaves the dead in their uncleanness, and therefore keeps at a distance from them, because it cannot remedy them; but Christ, having power to raise the dead . . . therefore is not shy of touching them.[8]

Once again, Jesus did the unexpected, and in his mercy and power not only raised the girl to life (which he could have done simply by saying a word) but also took her by the hand, technically defiling himself with yet another unclean person.

It reminds me of his willingness to go to the cross, bearing the sin and contamination of a world of sinners, so that all who believe in him might find forgiveness and everlasting life.

What was going on at the house when Jesus, Jairus, and the disciples arrived? Mayhem. The noise and confusion were deafening. Matthew, in his telling of the story, records that flute players were already there, and all three writers tell of loud weeping, wailing, and commotion. I am assuming that Jesus arrived shortly after the girl had died; already the ritual of mourning was in full swing. Another commentary note gives some insight into ancient funeral pageantry, which helped me picture the scene a little more clearly.

> In the ancient world, paid professional mourners (Matt. 9:23), most often women, aided families in their public expression of grief upon the death of a loved one. They composed poems or dirges praising the deceased, which they chanted to the accompaniment of a flute or other musical instrument in an attempt to stir the audience emotionally. They usually wore sack cloth and scattered dust in their hair and on their heads. Weeping, wailing, and beating their breasts, they created an unmistakable tone of grief.[9]

Mourning the dead was not subdued or respectfully quiet! To Jesus, who knew he would be raising the girl to vibrant life in a few moments, this synthetic grief was sickening, and he asked the mourners what all the fuss was about, since the girl wasn't dead but rather sleeping. The Scripture says that the noisy crowd (many of whom were likely being paid to weep for the girl) mocked him to scorn.

It's hard to imagine Jesus, who had just healed the hemorrhaging woman and countless others before her, being mocked. It would not be the last time he would endure such treatment, but in this instance he took control of the situation and gave instructions for everyone to be put out of the house, except for the girl's parents and three of his disciples, Peter, James, and John.

Then they entered the room where the girl lay. Taking her by the hand, Jesus spoke to her and told her to get up. In Luke 8:55 it is recorded that the girl's "spirit came again" (KJV) and that she got up immediately. Jesus told them to give her something to eat, thus showing that the child was no ghost.

How can this story apply to your life?

God is still willing to listen and help. Both Jairus and the hemorrhaging woman humbled themselves and poured out their hearts to Jesus. Does it take a crisis in your life to bring you to the point of seeking God's help? Sometimes it takes reaching "bottom" for some people to be willing to reach "up," and a personal crisis may cause us to break with our traditions and seek help. First Peter 5:7 reminds us to "cast all your anxiety on him because he cares for you."

God still honors the faith of those who seek his help. Are you trusting God for the future and seeking his help in times of need? He can give you peace and joy for today and hope for tomorrow.

I'm so grateful that whether God chooses to miraculously heal those I care about in this lifetime or in eternity, "wholeness" is a guarantee that awaits those of us who have put our faith in Jesus Christ (Rev. 21:4–5).

God offered compassion, mercy, and healing to many "untouchables" throughout his ministry, and we can do the same today. We live in a time when many are considered untouchable. The most drastic examples might be those suffering with AIDS, SARS, or leprosy. But what about others who are struggling with homelessness, divorce, depression, or an addiction? Do you avoid people with problems and treat them as untouchables? It's pretty unconvincing to say that we love and serve God when we reject individuals in need. The Bible says in Matthew 25:44–45: "'Lord, when did we see you hungry or thirsty or a stranger or needing clothes or sick or in prison, and did not help you?' He will reply, 'I tell you the truth, whatever you did not do for one of the least of these, you did not do for me.'"

HE WAS SO SICK. My healthy, active husband had come home from his JAG corps office at Fort Polk, Louisiana, desperately ill. My hand against his flushed face confirmed my suspicion of a high fever. As I helped him to our bed, he suddenly doubled over in pain and headed for the bathroom. What was this debilitating illness?

For a week I nursed him faithfully, until I suddenly became desperately ill myself. As the week progressed, my condition worsened to the point of near helplessness, and my husband, who was by then somewhat better, managed to get me to the hospital emergency room on base. Diagnosis: shigella, a nasty, highly contagious infection that causes severe abdominal pain and dysentery.

Weak, dehydrated, and contagious, I was placed in an isolation room with a warning sign posted above the door. No visitors allowed. Just outside the entrance to my room was a "decontamination station," where any personnel leaving my room had to sanitize themselves before going on with other duties. At first I was too sick to realize or even care about what was going on in the hallway, but by the fourth day in isolation, I was well enough to be aware. It was then that I fully realized what it meant to be "unclean."

In my extreme weakness I was very grateful for every kindness or assistance given to me, but while lying in that bed, I began to realize that some of the hospital personnel assigned to my care avoided me as much as possible. One nurse in particular was cold and abrupt; following each of her perfunctory visits, I could hear her vigorously scrubbing her hands and arms at the decontamination station outside. One day I heard her irritated voice say, "I hate going in there! I can hardly stand to breathe in that room, let alone touch her!"

I was shocked. Did she think I was deaf as well as sick? I knew I looked bad. I was thin, drawn, and wore no makeup—all factors that didn't help my self-esteem any. I understood I was contagious, but to be shunned and treated as if I had no feelings was devastating.

As her words sunk in, my emotions, which seemed as fragile as the rest of my body, crumbled. Tears started streaming from the corners of my eyes and pooled in my ears. Just as a sob escaped, my doctor stepped into the room. Seeing my tears and blotchy face, he asked me what was the matter.

"No one . . . wants to . . . come in here," I blubbered. "I can hear them talking in the hallway. Nobody even wants to touch me!"

I will never forget what that doctor did next. Instead of standing beside me as he usually did, he pulled a chair close to the bed, took both of my hands in his, and simply held them. "Jennie," he said, "I'm not afraid to touch you. Look, I'm holding your hands."

Seeing his genuine smile and feeling those hands holding mine seemed as comforting as a mother kissing her toddler's scraped knee. I laughed and cried at the same time.

Handing me a tissue, he grinned and gave me good news. "You're much better, you know, and I think you'll be able to go home tomorrow. For a few days you'll still feel like you've been run over by a truck, but by the time you come back to see me in a week, you'll be a whole new woman!"

My physician treated me with Christlike kindness that day, and I'll never forget it. The hard thing to remember is to reach out in kindness to others who may be desperate for God's loving touch in their lives.

A Whispered Prayer

Dear Heavenly Father, thank you for making yourself available to desperate people. Thank you for always being available and approachable when I come to you—desperate or not. Please help me to be more like you when spiritually, emotionally, or physically needy people cross my path in life or "interrupt" me when I'm busy. Give me wisdom to know how best to respond to each need, and most importantly, help me to introduce them to you, the one who can change their lives. In the precious name of Jesus, Amen.

Get Up and Go Ideas for Tomorrow

1. I will pray and ask God to open my eyes of compassion to the neediness of those around me.

2. I will drop off a bag of groceries at a local shelter or at the home of a newly widowed or divorced woman. I will let the recipient know that I am thinking of and praying for her.

3. If I know someone suffering from a debilitating illness, I will pray faithfully for him or her. I will show God's love by meeting a tangible need they may have, such as by volunteering my family to do yard work on a Saturday, and arriving with a casserole or a box of Krispy Kreme doughnuts!

A Thought to Ponder as I Fall Asleep

Who are the untouchables in my world? How can I respond to their needs with Christlikeness?

The Scripture Reading: Mark 5:21–43

When Jesus had again crossed over by boat to the other side of the lake, a large crowd gathered around him while he was by the lake. Then one of the synagogue rulers, named Jairus, came there. Seeing Jesus, he fell at his feet and pleaded earnestly with him, "My little daughter is dying. Please come and put your hands on her so that she will be healed and live." So Jesus went with him.

A large crowd followed and pressed around him. And a woman was there who had been subject to bleeding for twelve years. She had suffered a great deal under the care of many doctors and had spent all she had, yet instead of getting better she grew worse. When she heard about Jesus, she came up behind him in the crowd and touched his cloak, because she thought, "If I just touch

196

his clothes, I will be healed." Immediately her bleeding stopped and she felt in her body that she was freed from her suffering.

At once Jesus realized that power had gone out from him. He turned around in the crowd and asked, "Who touched my clothes?"

"You see the people crowding against you," his disciples answered, "and yet you can ask, 'Who touched me?'"

But Jesus kept looking around to see who had done it. Then the woman, knowing what had happened to her, came and fell at his feet and, trembling with fear, told him the whole truth. He said to her, "Daughter, your faith has healed you. Go in peace and be freed from your suffering."

While Jesus was still speaking, some men came from the house of Jairus, the synagogue ruler. "Your daughter is dead," they said. "Why bother the teacher any more?"

Ignoring what they said, Jesus told the synagogue ruler, "Don't be afraid; just believe."

He did not let anyone follow him except Peter, James and John the brother of James. When they came to the home of the synagogue ruler, Jesus saw a commotion, with people crying and wailing loudly. He went in and said to them, "Why all this commotion and wailing? The child is not dead but asleep." But they laughed at him.

After he put them all out, he took the child's father and mother and the disciples who were with him, and went in where the child was. He took her by the hand and said to her, *"Talitha koum!"* (which means, "Little girl, I say to you, get up!"). Immediately the girl stood up and walked around (she was twelve years old). At this they were completely astonished. He gave strict orders not to let anyone know about this, and told them to give her something to eat.

Final Note: Three New Testament writers give an account of the stories of Jairus's daughter and the hemorrhaging woman. For further study, read Matthew 9:18–26; Mark 5:22–43; and Luke 8:41–56.

NINE

Countdown to Mission Accomplished

Stories from the Final Week before Christ Died

W hat would I do?" My friend laughed at my question. "If I had just one week to live, I'd eat all the chocolate I wanted!" Then sobering a little, she added, "I'd surprise my husband at work with a picnic lunch and make sweet love to him at night. And I'd hug my kids a lot and make sure they knew their mom loved them." Her face lit up for a moment. "I read once about a mom who knew she was going to die of cancer, and she wrote letters ahead for each of her kids to open on every birthday. I'd like to do that. Oh, and I'd try to make sure the laundry was caught up," she added, her eyes suddenly watery.

She paused thoughtfully and then grimaced. "And I suppose I should forgive my brother-in-law." She sighed. "I haven't spoken to Mike for over a year—ever since he cheated on my sister. If she can forgive him, I suppose I should be able to. I guess I should ask God to forgive me for a number of other infractions as well. And speaking of God, I think I'd pray and ask if he'd postpone my deadline. A week really wouldn't be enough time to get ready." She shook her head and then brightened as another idea came to her. "And if he couldn't give me an extension, I'd ask if my death could be instantaneous so I could enjoy life up until the last moment. I'm not very good with pain." She gave a huge sigh. "Whew, that was a tough one! What brought that question on, anyway?"

I chuckled but then explained that I had been studying some of the events that took place leading up to the crucifixion of Jesus. "He knew it was his last week," I commented, "and he knew exactly how devastating and painful it would be. But rather than zap his enemies or leave the country, or earth for that matter, and avoid ridicule, abuse, and a brutal crucifixion, the Son of God lived through each day, each moment, fulfilling Old Testament prophecy and ultimately allowing himself to be crucified, sacrificing himself for the sin of the world."

IT WOULD BE IMPOSSIBLE to adequately tell the entire story of that week in just one chapter of *More Night Whispers*, so in the following pages, I'm going to share some poignant "snapshots" from those days, incorporating details I learned about some of the characters that took part in the drama, and including portions of the story from all four of the Gospel writers.

200

Six Days before the Tomb

It was Sunday, and the dusty streets were crowded with pilgrims from across the country of Judea and beyond, filling the city of Jerusalem to overflowing in preparation for Passover, which was one of the most sacred Jewish holidays.

It made Pilate nervous. Looking out over the swelling city from a palace balcony, the Roman governor of Judea swept his gaze over the throng of people making their way through the streets, and then took in the sight of the magnificent temple with its massive columns and courtyards. He and his wife had traveled from their palace in Caesarea to Jerusalem specifically for the Passover. This was the time when riots and political uprisings were most likely, and he wanted to be on hand to keep things under control.

They're a rebellious bunch, he thought with distaste, wishing for the hundredth time that he had been given a more prestigious post by the Roman government. The Jews had never accepted being conquered by Rome, and the religious leaders were constantly making demands of him. Pilate found it annoying to bow to some of those demands, but he had no choice; he feared the religious leaders' power to influence the people to riot. Word might get back to Rome that he couldn't control his subjects.

With a disgusted shake of his head, he left the heat of the balcony for the cool interior of the palace.

"HERE HE COMES!" a man called out. Adults and children alike pressed forward to see. Over the past three years, many had listened as Jesus taught in Judea, Galilee, and beyond. Stories of his miracles had spread like wildfire across the region, and the popular rabbi drew crowds and brought hope to people wherever he went. On that Sunday, as Jesus made his triumphant entry into the city on a donkey, his disciples called out jubilantly as they walked beside him, and Passover pilgrims lined the roadway, waving palm branches and calling out, "Blessed is he who comes in the name of the Lord!"

But by Monday, not all the Jews were cheering. Standing in his own palatial quarters, Caiaphas, the Jewish high priest and president of the Sanhedrin, the ruling religious council, gritted his teeth as he listened to numerous reports from other leaders in the Jewish council.

"Jesus rode into town and was received like a king!" one said with disgust.

"The people were worshiping him, shouting, 'Hosannah!' and 'Blessed is he who comes in the name of the Lord!'" offered another. "His popularity may be unstoppable."

"I've heard enough!" Caiaphas yelled. "He's a dangerous troublemaker!"

Jesus had been so bold as to go into the temple and throw out the money changers, saying they had violated the house of God. And ever since he had raised Lazarus from the dead just a few miles away in Bethany, his popularity had increased. Caiaphas couldn't let that continue.

"If the people get out of hand because of him, it could bring Rome down upon our heads. He must be eliminated. Do you understand me? Dead!"

On Tuesday, when Jesus was teaching in Jerusalem, a group of Pharisees cornered him, demanding that he explain what gave him the authority to do the things he did. To their frustration, Jesus evaded the verbal traps of the religious leaders, recognizing that they were trying to get him to contradict Moses and discredit himself in front of the crowd that had gathered. All day long, he dealt with people, teaching, telling parables, answering questions. On Wednesday, he rested in Bethany.

"JESUS IS SMART, I'll grant him that," Caiaphas admitted to the chief priests and elders who had gathered in his home. "We must come up with a plan to kill him without alarming the crowds who follow him. We don't need a riot on our hands during Passover while so many people are in the city."

A servant approached the high priest to tell him he had a visitor. Surprise, and then a slow, calculating smile lit the priest's fleshy face. After instructing the servant to admit the man into the room, he turned to the council before him. "This should be most interesting."

A lean man stepped into the room with an anxious but determined look and approached Caiaphas. A slight murmur of surprise swept the council as those present recognized the fellow as a follower of Jesus—and not just any follower. This man was Judas Iscariot, one of the twelve disciples closest to Jesus.

"Do you know who I am?" the man asked.

"I believe I do," Caiaphas said, feigning boredom.

"Then I'll get right to the point. What are you willing to give me if I hand him over to you?"

Caiaphas almost choked on his own spit. Recovering, he glanced toward his chief counselors before narrowing his eyes. "I am assuming we are discussing the troublemaker called Jesus?"

"You know we are."

"Well, then." Caiaphas was fully himself again, and his calculating mind was working overtime. "I'm not sure that we need any help to deal with the man, but I suppose I could consult with the council on this small matter." He turned to the others in the room. "Shall we pay him thirty silver coins to hand over Jesus to us?" Caiaphas knew this sum was the price of a mere slave.

Doubt flickered over the face of Judas for a moment, and then resolve. Caiaphas, enjoying Judas's disappointment, couldn't conceal a small smirk.

"All right, then," Judas agreed. "I'll let you know when the time is right."

JESUS LOOKED AROUND the room at the men he had chosen to follow him over the past three years—the men he had mentored, taught, and trained to carry on his work. All but one would carry on his name and ministry. How he loved them all.

It was Thursday evening, and they had gathered together for the Feast of Unleavened Bread in preparation for Passover. Jesus had sent Peter and John ahead earlier that day to secure the upstairs meeting room and to prepare for the Passover meal. The ceremonial meal involved sacrificing a lamb at the temple and eating it while sitting around a table with one's family.[1] That's what they had become—a family—and as he looked at each of them around the table, he knew this was the last supper they would have together. He knew that each of them would be faced with their own failures before the night was over. And he knew it would be the longest, hardest night of his life.

Did they understand he would die the next day and that the kingdom of God would be in heaven? No, and to prove their spiritual immaturity, they started arguing about who among them would be the greatest in the new kingdom.

With a sigh, Jesus got up, wrapped a towel around his waist, and poured water into a bowl. Then, kneeling down, he reached toward one who had been arguing and began to wash his feet.

The disciples glanced at each other in shock, raising their eyebrows as if to say, "Foot washing is the work of women and servants, certainly not a chore for the Master!" When Jesus came to Peter, the disciple pulled his foot from Jesus' grasp, saying that Jesus would *never* wash his feet. Jesus simply reached for the foot again, teaching a lesson in humility and love.

When Jesus was finished, he sat down again and said, "I'm speaking the truth when I tell you that one of you who is sitting at this table will betray me."

The disciples again looked at each other in shock. They began murmuring to each other and then saying to Jesus, "It won't be me, will it, Lord? Surely not me."

JUDAS SWALLOWED HARD and looked away from Jesus. But Jesus would not take his eyes off him.

"I, the Son of Man, will die, just as it has been written, but woe to the one who betrays me," Jesus said sadly. Picking up a piece of bread, he dipped it in a bowl of olive oil and handed it to Judas. "What you are about to do, do quickly," he said.

The others at the table had begun talking among themselves again. Since Judas was the treasurer of the group, they thought Jesus was telling him to go out and buy something that was needed for the feast.

But Judas knew. Taking the bread, he left them and headed to Caiaphas.

When he was gone, Jesus told the other disciples that he would only be with them a little while longer. "Where I'm going, you can't go," Jesus told them, "but you will follow later." (He was referring to heaven, but they did not know that.)

"But Lord, why can't I follow you?" Peter asked. "I would lay down my life for you!"

"Would you, Peter? Believe me when I tell you now that before the rooster crows tomorrow morning, you will have denied me three times."

Peter couldn't believe his ears. He would never deny Jesus. Would he?

Darkness had fallen by the time they walked to the Garden of Gethsemane, a familiar and peaceful place where they had often gone before. Jesus asked his disciples to pray while he went apart from them and agonized in prayer himself, wrestling with the knowledge of what lay ahead and then submitting to what he knew was the Father's will.

Three times he went back to his disciples and found them asleep. He roused them the third time, announcing that his hour was near. In the distance, Jesus could hear a commotion. Soon lanterns appeared through the trees, and Judas arrived with armed soldiers and a mob that included members of Caiaphas's vast household staff.

When Judas kissed Jesus on the cheek, someone in the crowd yelled, "Get him!" and chaos erupted. Guards surged forward to arrest Jesus, and Peter wildly brandished his sword at the aggressors and roared "No!" before slicing off a guard's ear.

Jesus stopped Peter with a quiet word, reached to heal the man's wound, and said to his disciples, "Don't you realize that I can call on my Father, and he will at once put thousands of angels at my disposal?"

After that, the mob surged forward to take Jesus, and his frightened disciples fled in every direction.

During that night and the early hours of the following morning, Jesus was taken to six different hearings. After first being hustled off for questioning at the home of Annas, Caiaphas's father-in-law, he was taken to the palace of Caiaphas, where a religious trial before some of the teachers of the law and the elders was hastily convened. This took place during the middle of the night; without legal representation, Jesus was badgered, questioned, and scorned as the religious leaders desperately tried to find some legal ground on which to charge him that would warrant the death penalty. The religious leaders called many prearranged false witnesses, but the testimonies conflicted with each other. Jesus simply remained silent.

Caiaphas was tired and angry, and in a burst of fury he finally snarled, "Aren't you going to defend yourself against the charges of these witnesses?" Rising to his feet and stomping up to where Jesus had been forced to stand bound for hours, he shouted, "I charge you under oath by the living God: Tell us if you are the Christ, the Son of God!"

"Yes," Jesus said, and then he raised his voice so all could hear, "and in the future you will see me sitting at the right hand of the Father and coming on the clouds of heaven."

A guard struck him, and Jesus' head snapped back, blood spurting from his lip.

"Blasphemy!" Caiaphas shouted as he reached for the neck of his own robe and dramatically tore it down the front. "Why do we need any more witnesses?"

Two of Jesus' disciples witnessed what happened. John had slipped in and watched helplessly from the crowd in the back. And there was Judas, the betrayer, who has having second thoughts. Outside, a third disciple had made his way into the courtyard and was warming himself nervously at a fire there. Recognized by some who had seen him before with Jesus, Peter denied even knowing Christ three times before the rooster heralded the dawn of the new day.

The entire Jewish council met together soon after daybreak, and they formally approved the decision of the "secret session" in order to make the proceedings appear legal before Jesus was sent to Pilate for sentencing.

When he saw what they had done, Judas came forward and threw the money they had given him on the ground. "I have sinned," he cried, "for I have betrayed innocent blood!"

"What is that to us?" the council responded with contempt. Judas left them and hung himself.

THE MORNING DAWNED hot and dry. Pilate stepped out on his balcony to catch a breath of air before beginning a grueling festival day. He clenched his fist when he saw a mob coming toward him from the direction of Caiaphas's palace. Irritated, he motioned for them to enter the courtyard below. To his disgust, the priests refused to enter because of possible contamination before their Passover. What strange rules those Jews had. He couldn't believe he actually had to go out to meet *them*.

He was so irritated that when they pushed a bound and somewhat battered man forward and requested his judgment, he shouted, "Why are you disturbing me with this matter? Take him yourselves and judge him by your own law."

"But we have no authority to execute anyone!" someone in the mob said.

Suddenly suspicious and wondering what they were up to, Pilate motioned for the prisoner to be brought to him for questioning.

Pilate eyed the bound man who stood before him with quiet dignity. *Unusual fellow, this Jesus,* he thought to himself. The prisoner didn't say much, but he had penetrating eyes that made Pilate nervous.

"Don't you hear the testimony they're bringing against you?" he asked Jesus, who in turn remained silent. "What is it you've done?" Pilate persisted. Then with a slight smirk he asked, "Are you really the king of the Jews?"

Jesus finally answered him, quietly and calmly. "Yes, what you say is truth, but my kingdom is not of this world. If it were, my servants would fight to prevent my arrest by the Jews, but my kingdom is from another place."

"What is truth, anyway?" Pilate responded with a cynical shrug. Feeling uneasy about the matter, he decided to get out of the situation by passing the affair right back to the Jewish authorites. He sent Jesus to Herod Agrippa, who was in town for the Passover. Herod was the Jewish king, appointed by the Roman government.

"WELL, LOOK WHAT THE DOGS dragged in," Herod chuckled when a bound and bedraggled Jesus was brought to him on Friday morning. "I don't usually schedule entertainment before breakfast, but then, I don't usually have helpless miracle workers here either." He laughed. "Listen, teacher, if you want mercy from me, the show had better be good!"

Hoping to be amused or even amazed by a "miracle," Herod soon lost patience when Jesus stood mute and did nothing. So he mocked and ridiculed the prisoner. Herod's soldiers took their cue from the king and relieved their boredom with persecution. When they tired of their cruel games, they sent Jesus back to the governor.

PILATE EYED THE PRISONER, noting that he was worse for wear. He had obviously been beaten. *He's an innocent man with very powerful enemies. But he doesn't deserve to die.*

The fact that the enemies of Jesus had caused Pilate his own share of problems made him even more interested in thwarting the wishes of the Jews. Seeing Jesus bruised and bloodied gave him a cruel idea that he thought might actually work in Jesus' favor. Calling his guards, he gave the order for Jesus to be flogged. "Make sure it shows," he instructed grimly. *Perhaps when they feel he's been properly punished for his crime, they'll take pity on the man.*

IT DIDN'T WORK. When the guards produced Jesus to the mob, he was almost unrecognizable. The whip had done its job—under his blood-soaked garment, bone had been exposed. Pilate found the sight of the man almost nauseating, with his bloody head, swollen jaw, and one eye swollen shut. The prisoner was draped in a "royal" robe for his presentation, once elegant but ruined by stain and sweat. And that ludicrous crown. The soldiers may have meant it to be funny, but Pilate couldn't help but wince when he saw the size of the thorns and the damage they had caused to Jesus' skull.

"Here is the man," Pilate called to the crowd as he gestured toward the pitiful figure who could barely stand.

"Crucify him!" came a shout from the crowd, and others joined in the chorus.

"I am telling you that I find no basis for a charge against him," Pilate shouted back. "The man has been thoroughly flogged. Look, he's almost dead already. You have a custom that one prisoner may be released during the Passover. I give you a choice. Shall I free Jesus, who is called Christ, or Barabbas?" Pilate thought he'd fooled them then; Barabbas was a notorious terrorist who was guilty of murder.

But the crowd surprised him. "Barabbas!" they shouted. "Crucify Jesus!"

"But why? What crime has he committed?" Pilate shouted in frustration. But he knew he was getting nowhere; instead, an uproar was starting.

In exasperation, the governor of Judea gave in. He called for water and a towel, and before the crowd he washed his hands. "I am innocent of this man's blood," he said. "It is your responsibility."

A haunting cry came back from the crowd. "Let his blood be on us and on our children!"

Barabbas was released, and Jesus was handed over to be crucified.

It was still early, and the rest of the city, with its quadrupled population, was just waking up when the procession to the Place of the Skull began. The spectacle drew a crowd as Jesus, bloodied and bowed under the weight of the heavy crossbeam, moved slowly through the street. Passover pilgrims stared in horror, and those whose lives Jesus had touched, healed, and changed cried out in despair. He had rescued so many from impossible situations. Why didn't he save himself?

At 9:00 a.m. Jesus Christ was crucified. Disregarding the open wounds on his back, the soldiers stripped the prisoner and pushed him down on the ground, where they stretched his arms over the crossbeam. His body jerked violently as spikes were driven through his hands. To the guards' surprise, he did not cry out. After he was pinned to the beam, the soldiers lifted it to fit into a large notch in the upright post that stood standing ready for its burden. Once Jesus was hanging upright, the soldiers drove spikes through his feet and into the post.

The soldiers were busy that morning—they had two other prisoners to crucify as well. While the two thieves cursed and struggled, Jesus was quiet, suffering, struggling to breathe. But he did manage to say something that surprised the hardened men.

"Father, forgive them. They don't know what they do."

"Did you hear what that fellow said?" one soldier remarked to another. "Do you think he was talking about us?"

"Maybe," another executioner said. "Quite the gentleman, isn't he?" He laughed. "Hey, look at this." He held up Jesus' garment. "There's not a seam in this thing. Let's not cut this up. I'd rather gamble for the chance of getting the whole thing."

THE CROSSES HAD BEEN PLANTED close to the road, and those passing by mocked the dying. The religious rulers, satisfied that they had accomplished their purpose, stopped before the cross to examine Christ in his seeming helplessness. "He saved others; let him save himself if he is the Christ of God, the Chosen One," they sneered. Even the robbers hanging beside him called out insults.

As the hours dragged by, muscle spasms seized the victims, and breathing became more and more difficult. The insults of one of the prisoners changed to a plea for Jesus to allow him to enter into the Kingdom of Heaven after his death. Jesus pushed up on his feet to get a gasp of air. "Today," he rasped out painfully, "today you will be with me in paradise."

Insects swarmed around them, feasting on open wounds.

SEVERAL WEEPING WOMEN, accompanied by one man, pressed closer to the cross. Other women who had faithfully followed and supported Jesus' ministry watched and wept from a distance.

John was there, supporting the arm of Mary, the mother of Jesus. Her sister was also with her, as was Mary Magdalene. Jesus' mother's anguish at the sight of her son's suffering was unbearable. She felt as if a sword had lodged itself in her own heart. Her precious son—God's Son—dying? How she longed to cover his nakedness, to wash the encrusted blood from his body, to sooth his wounded brow. Did he even realize she was there? She swallowed to rid her throat of the painful lump and haltingly started repeating aloud a psalm she knew he loved.

SUDDENLY THE SKY GREW DARK. Startled by the difference in light and temperature after the heat of the unrelenting noonday sun, people studied the heavens and shivered in the strange twilight. What was this—an eclipse?

For three hours darkness covered the sky. The shouting and mocking quieted, and the crowd thinned as some hastily retreated from Golgotha, the Place of the Skull, for the security of their own homes. The soldiers standing guard at the cross eyed the sky and shuffled uneasily at their post. And then came the haunting cry some would remember their whole lives.

"My God! My God! Why . . . have you forsaken me?"

The wail echoed in the darkness.

A PEACE CAME OVER the tortured body. His work here was completed. It was 3:00, the time for afternoon sacrifices. He could go *home*. The price was paid.

One last triumphant cry pierced the air.

"It is . . . *finished*! Father, into thy hands . . . I commit . . . my spirit."

A tremor shook the tortured body, and his head dropped limply against his chest. With that, the Savior died.

Digging Deeper

He was pierced for our transgressions, he was crushed for our iniquities; the punishment that brought us peace was upon him, and by his wounds we are healed. . . . The LORD has laid on him the iniquity of us all.

Isaiah 53:5–6

213

Jesus Christ came into the world to accomplish a specific purpose. His name, Jesus, means "God is Savior," which de-scribes exactly who he was and is. "*Christ* is the New Testament equivalent of *Messiah*, a Hebrew word meaning 'anointed one,'"[2] which referred to the fact that "Jesus was divinely appointed to His mission, and that He had an official relationship to God the Father."[3]

While much of the story of the crucifixion is heartbreaking, Christ's death gives Christians freedom from impossibly cum-bersome laws, and his resurrection literally guarantees believers' victory over death! Discussing every aspect of the story would take more than an entire book, but let's take a closer look at the custom of ritual sacrifice and at some of the interesting characters we met as the story unfolded. And, by the way, if you think I've discounted the role of some important females, just wait till the next chapter!

Why were animals sacrificed at the temple? To us, as twenty-first-century people reading the Bible, it seems as if the people in the Old Testament were continually making sacrifices. A study note in the Life Application Bible explains the old covenant, or solemn agreement, that God had with his people. (You can look up the references given for greater understanding.)

> In Old Testament times, God agreed to forgive people's sins if they brought animals for the priests to sacrifice. When this sacrificial system was inaugurated, the agreement between God and man was sealed with the blood of animals (Exod. 24:8).
>
> But animal blood did not in itself remove sin (only God can forgive sin), and animal sacrifices had to be repeated day by day and year after year. Jesus instituted a "new covenant" or agreement between humans and God. Under this new covenant, Jesus would

die in the place of sinners. Unlike the blood of animals, his blood (because he is God) would truly remove the sins of all who put their faith in him. And Jesus' sacrifice would never have to be repeated; it would be good for all eternity (Heb. 9:23–28).[4]

Why did Jesus get passed around to so many officials before he was crucified? Jews, while under the control of Rome, were allowed to have their own court system to deal with infractions regarding religious matters. There were two major religious groups: the Pharisees, who were considered "legalists" and were fanatic about religious tradition, and the Sadducees, who denied life after death, among other things that Jesus taught. The Sadducees were the greater power brokers, and many of them served on the Sanhedrin, which was the religious supreme court. Both groups had joined forces to deal with Jesus.

Their problem was that they wanted Jesus dead by the most disgusting and humiliating manner possible, but the Jews were not allowed to sentence people to crucifixion. That fell under Roman authority and was usually used as punishment for slaves and political/military criminals.

So starting in the middle of the night, after Caiaphas's mob arrested Jesus, the Jewish leaders convened an illegal trial and reached a decision just after daybreak. From there they brought Jesus to Pilate, the Roman governor, who wanted nothing to do with the matter. Pilate sent Jesus to Herod, the Jewish king who owed his throne to Rome. Herod mocked Jesus and gave him to the Roman guards to make sport of him before sending him back to Pilate, who, after having Jesus flogged, finally washed his hands of the matter and gave the Jewish leaders what they wanted: a Roman execution. This all happened before 9:00 a.m. on Friday morning, when Jesus was crucified. Can you imagine such a night . . . such a morning . . . such a day?

Who played politics in this story? The culprits include Annas, Herod, and Judas, but the major political players in this story are Caiaphas and Pilate, who couldn't stand each other.

Caiaphas was the Jewish high priest and had major authority over his fellow Jews. *Fausset's Bible Dictionary* tells us that he was in office from AD 26–37. "Unscrupulous vigour, combined with political shrewdness, characterizes him in the New Testament, as it also kept him in office longer than any of his predecessors."[5]

What saddens and angers me as I think of Caiaphas is that, as the highest "church" leader, he was thoroughly schooled in Old Testament prophecy and should have been looking for the promised Messiah. Fausset comments that "the priesthood at the time no longer comprehended the end of their own calling."[6] Protecting his own position and power base was far more important to Caiaphas than accepting God's promised Savior as the final sacrifice. He disregarded the fact that God had a master plan, foretold generations before.

Pilate was appointed the sixth governor of Judea by Tiberius in AD 25 or 26,[7] which means that he and Caiaphas came into their respective positions of power at approximately the same time. I found it interesting to learn that Pilate's job was usually given to "a Roman knight, acting . . . as a collector of revenue, and judge in cases arising under it. Pontius Pilate had full military and judicial authority in Judea."[8] The ancient historian Josephus reported that Pilate's relationship with the Jews was rough from the start, and on several occasions his actions deeply offended them, resulting in riots. At times Pilate despised the frustrating job he had been given, and when the "Jesus matter" showed up on his doorstep early one Friday morning, it probably seemed like one more headache.

The Life Application Bible concisely describes Pilate's position at that time.

> For Pilate, there was never a doubt about Jesus' innocence. Three separate times he declared Jesus not guilty. He couldn't understand what made these people want to kill Jesus, but his fear of the pressure the Jews would place on him made him decide to allow Jesus' crucifixion. Because of the people's threat to inform the emperor that Pilate hadn't eliminated a rebel against Rome, Pilate went against what he knew was right. In desperation, he chose to do wrong.[9]

Did all the Jewish religious leaders hate Jesus? No. There were some who were drawn to him and what he had to say. (Remember Jairus in Capernaum?) Others were "closet Christians," that is, they were well aware of Old Testament prophecy and believed that Jesus was the promised Messiah, but they had not made their faith public. Nor did their voices carry as much authority as that of Caiaphas, who was a self-serving master manipulator.

What was the crucifixion actually like? It was terrible. Researching it made me weep.

We know from the account of Matthew that Jesus was "scourged" or whipped with a flagellum. This was a whip made of leather straps weighted at the tips with sharp pieces of metal or bone; when the whip struck, often wrapping around the body, it would tear the flesh. Sometimes beatings were so severe that bone was exposed, causing severe blood loss. Jesus also endured repeated blows to the head after bring "crowned" with a circle of large thorns that were pushed into his skull. Then he was paraded to the execution site but was unable to carry his cross the entire way, most likely because of exhaustion and blood loss.

A Bible manners and customs book filled in some of the other questions I had in my mind about what a crucifixion victim had to endure.

As part of his shame he was forced to carry his cross—not the whole cross, only the crossbeam. The upright part was permanently installed at the site . . . and had a groove into which the crossbeam could be inserted. . . . Someone would precede him carrying the sign . . . indicating the crime of which he was guilty. All along the way bystanders could ridicule him. They stripped the prisoner of his clothing on reaching the place of crucifixion. This was part of his shame, and there was no consideration of niceties. Then his arms were attached to the crossbeams. They could be tied but were often nailed—through the hands or wrists. Scripture indicates that Jesus was nailed to the cross.

Now they inserted the crossbeam into the upright post. A peg or ledge halfway up the upright . . . helped to support the body. The legs could be tied . . . or nailed. If nailed, a nail might be driven through each foot or ankle as the legs were extended down. . . . Alternately the body might be turned sideways, the knees bent, and the one foot put on top of the other so a single nail could be driven through both feet. . . . If there was an accusation they nailed that above the head of the victim. . . .

They left the crucified one to die, the feet of the victim only a few inches from the ground, not high in the air, as is often portrayed in artwork. He suffered greatly, including the taunts and indignities of passersby, the exposure to heat and cold and insects (sometimes animals). He suffered the pain of wounds, often infected, and the intense thirst. Depending on the strength of one's constitution, death might be prolonged but usually took at least thirty-six hours.[10]

Fausset described the agony:

(1) the unnatural position of the body, causing pain at the least motion; (2) the nails being driven through the hands and feet, which are full of nerves and tendons, yet without a vital part being directly injured; (3) the wounds so long exposed bringing on acute inflammation and gangrene; (4) the distended parts causing more blood to flow through the arteries than can be carried back through the veins; (5) the lingering anguish and burning thirst.[11]

You've read more than enough, right? And you're probably wondering why I gave you so much detail. Well, I'm afraid that in the past I have sat through so many Good Friday services and Easter cantatas (wearing new outfits, of course) that I was "conditioned" to the point that the services rarely moved me. I wonder if you have experienced the same. I will never attend such a service again without "seeing" his pain, and I hope you won't either. How offensive my ignorant indifference must have seemed to the One who suffered so greatly on that cross for me.

How can you apply this story to your life?

Recognize what Jesus Christ did for you personally on the cross and accept him as your Savior. To learn about the story of Jesus' life and death is one thing, but to accept it for yourself is a life-altering act of faith. The religious leaders during Bible times who knew all about Old Testament law and prophecy were full of "head" knowledge, but the majority of them never came to realize that God's promises were being fulfilled in their own lifetime. Don't settle for knowing *about* Jesus when he invites you to know him

219

personally. The Bible says, "He came unto his own, and they that were his own received him not. But as many as received him, to them gave he the right to become children of God, *even* to them that believe on his name" (John 1:11–12 ASV).

When facing difficult situations, follow the example of Jesus. The night before he was crucified, Jesus suffered dread and great anxiety over what lay ahead of him. He did three things that we would do well to follow when we face difficult times in our lives:

- he sought to be with friends who were believers
- he spent meaningful time in prayer
- he determined to do the will of his heavenly Father

Deliberately do what you know is right (in spite of pressure from people around you to do otherwise). Pilate knew what was right, but he chose to do wrong. Pilate was as human as we are, and although he was in a position of great power and authority, he allowed himself to be manipulated by evil men. Someone said, "He had his moment in history, and now we have ours." Do you use the opportunities that come your way to promote yourself or to glorify Christ?

IN REFLECTING ON THE POWERFUL STORY of Jesus' sacrificial death, I am reminded of a story that my sister, author and speaker Carol Kent, often shares at the close of her testimony. Here it is in her own words.

Years ago I heard the story of a missionary who was serving the Lord in Korea. A young Korean woman was expecting a baby, and on Christmas Eve she went into labor. There was a major storm in progress, but the woman knew if she could just get to the home of the missionary, she would have the help she so desperately needed to bring her baby into the world. She put on her winter wraps and started out alone, on foot. She was several miles from home when her labor pains grew in frequency and intensity, and she knew she could not make it to her destination.

She got beneath an old bridge that afforded a bit of shelter. There, alone, in the middle of the night, she gave birth to a beautiful baby boy. She immediately removed her coat and then, piece by piece, the rest of her clothing. Carefully, she wound every item around her baby until he looked like a cumbersome cocoon. Then she fell asleep, too exhausted to do anything else.

The next morning brightly dawned, and the missionary awoke with a song in her heart. It was Christmas Day, and there were so many people she wanted to see. She packed her car and started on her way. A few miles down the road the engine sputtered, and the car finally stopped on top of an old bridge. As the missionary opened the door to go for help, she thought she heard a baby crying. Following the sound, she went under the bridge where she found a tiny baby boy—very hungry, but very much alive. Next to the infant lay his mother—frozen.

The missionary picked up the baby and took him to her home. In time, she was permitted to adopt the boy. As the years passed, she told him how his biological mother had given her life that he might live. Her son never tired of hearing the story, and he asked her to repeat it again and again.

On his twelfth birthday he asked the missionary to take him to the burial place of his mother. When they arrived, there was snow on the ground, and he asked his missionary mother to wait while he went to the graveside alone. She watched her son as he trudged through the snow, tears streaming down his cheeks. In amazement, she saw him slowly unbutton his coat, remove it, and gently lay it on the snowy grave. Next he removed his shirt, trousers, shoes, and socks and carefully placed each item on the grave of the mother who had given her all for him.

The missionary could take it no longer and went to her son, placing her coat around his bare, shivering shoulders. Through his tears, she heard him as he asked, "Were you colder than this for me, Mother?" And he knew that she was.

That's a beautiful picture of what the Lord Jesus Christ did for you and me. The Bible explains that He left heaven's glory to come to this earth. He came in complete obedience to His Father's will to give His life that you and I might experience forgiveness of sin and eternal life by trusting Him as Savior and Lord.[12]

A Whispered Prayer

Dear Heavenly Father, thank you for being willing to send your own Son to suffer shame and to die a horrific death on the cross of Calvary in order to provide a final payment for sin for whoever believes in him. I admit that I am a sinner and that I don't deserve this great sacrifice. Thank you for forgiving my sins and for the home in heaven I will have with you in eternity. In the precious name of Jesus, Amen.

Get Up and Go Ideas for Tomorrow

1. I will take time to read Isaiah 52 and 53 and look for verses that foretold how the Messiah would suffer.
2. I will explain what I have learned about this powerful story to someone else.

A Thought to Ponder As I Fall Asleep

When was the last time I sincerely thanked Jesus for what he did for me on the cross?

The Scripture Reading: John 18:28–19:30

Then the Jews led Jesus from Caiaphas to the palace of the Roman governor. By now it was early morning, and to avoid ceremonial uncleanness the Jews did not enter the palace; they wanted to be able to eat the Passover. So Pilate came out to them and asked, "What charges are you bringing against this man?"

"If he were not a criminal," they replied, "we would not have handed him over to you."

Pilate said, "Take him yourselves and judge him by your own law."

"But we have no right to execute anyone," the Jews objected. This happened so that the words Jesus had spoken indicating the kind of death he was going to die would be fulfilled.

Pilate then went back inside the palace, summoned Jesus and asked him, "Are you the king of the Jews?"

"Is that your own idea," Jesus asked, "or did others talk to you about me?"

"Am I a Jew?" Pilate replied. "It was your people and your chief priests who handed you over to me. What is it you have done?"

Jesus said, "My kingdom is not of this world. If it were, my servants would fight to prevent my arrest by the Jews. But now my kingdom is from another place."

"You are a king, then!" said Pilate.

Jesus answered, "You are right in saying I am a king. In fact, for this reason I was born, and for this I came into the world, to testify to the truth. Everyone on the side of truth listens to me."

"What is truth?" Pilate asked. With this he went out again to the Jews and said, "I find no basis for a charge against him. But it is your custom for me to release to you one prisoner at the time of the Passover. Do you want me to release 'the king of the Jews'?"

They shouted back, "No, not him! Give us Barabbas!" Now Barabbas had taken part in a rebellion.

Then Pilate took Jesus and had him flogged. The soldiers twisted together a crown of thorns and put it on his head. They clothed him in a purple robe and went up to him again and again, saying, "Hail, king of the Jews!" And they struck him in the face.

Once more Pilate came out and said to the Jews, "Look, I am bringing him out to you to let you know that I find no basis for a charge against him." When Jesus came out wearing the crown of thorns and the purple robe, Pilate said to them, "Here is the man!"

As soon as the chief priests and their officials saw him, they shouted, "Crucify! Crucify!"

But Pilate answered, "You take him and crucify him. As for me, I find no basis for a charge against him."

The Jews insisted, "We have a law, and according to that law he must die, because he claimed to be the Son of God."

223

When Pilate heard this, he was even more afraid, and he went back inside the palace. "Where do you come from?" he asked Jesus, but Jesus gave him no answer. "Do you refuse to speak to me?" Pilate said. "Don't you realize I have power either to free you or to crucify you?"

Jesus answered, "You would have no power over me if it were not given to you from above. Therefore the one who handed me over to you is guilty of a greater sin."

From then on, Pilate tried to set Jesus free, but the Jews kept shouting, "If you let this man go, you are no friend of Caesar. Anyone who claims to be a king opposes Caesar."

When Pilate heard this, he brought Jesus out and sat down on the judge's seat at a place known as the Stone Pavement (which in Aramaic is Gabbatha). It was the day of Preparation of Passover Week, about the sixth hour.

"Here is your king," Pilate said to the Jews.

But they shouted, "Take him away! Take him away! Crucify him!"

"Shall I crucify your king?" Pilate asked.

"We have no king but Caesar," the chief priests answered.

Finally Pilate handed him over to them to be crucified.

So the soldiers took charge of Jesus. Carrying his own cross, he went out to the place of the Skull (which in Aramaic is called Golgotha). Here they crucified him, and with him two others—one on each side and Jesus in the middle.

Pilate had a notice prepared and fastened to the cross. It read: JESUS OF NAZARETH, THE KING OF THE JEWS. Many of the Jews read this sign, for the place where Jesus was crucified was near the city, and the sign was written in Aramaic, Latin and Greek. The chief priests of the Jews protested to Pilate, "Do not write 'the King of the Jews,' but that this man claimed to be king of the Jews."

Pilate answered, "What I have written, I have written."

When the soldiers crucified Jesus, they took his clothes, dividing them into four shares, one for each of them, with the undergarment remaining. This garment was seamless, woven in one piece from top to bottom.

"Let's not tear it," they said to one another. "Let's decide by lot who will get it."

This happened that the Scripture might be fulfilled which said,

> "They divided my garments among
>   them
>   and cast lots for my clothing."

So this is what the soldiers did.

Near the cross of Jesus stood his mother, his mother's sister, Mary the wife of Clopas, and Mary Magdalene. When Jesus saw his mother there, and the disciple whom he loved standing nearby, he said to his mother, "Dear woman, here is your son," and to the disciple, "Here is your mother." From that time on, this disciple took her into his home.

Later, knowing that all was now completed, and so that the Scripture would be fulfilled, Jesus said, "I am thirsty." A jar of wine vinegar was there, so they soaked a sponge in it, put the sponge on a stalk of the hyssop plant, and lifted it to Jesus' lips. When he had received the drink, Jesus said, "It is finished." With that, he bowed his head and gave up his spirit.

Final Note: The crucifixion of Jesus was recorded by all four Gospel writers, Matthew, Mark, Luke, and John, as well as by the Jewish historian Josephus. Details of this event were foretold by the Old Testament prophet Isaiah and others. (See Exodus 12:46; Numbers 9:12; Psalm 22:18, 34:20, 69:21; Zechariah 12:10, in addition to Isaiah 52–53, for further study.)

TEN

Aftershock and Awesome Joy

Stories of Men
and Women at
and after the Cross

On April 4, 1999, I sat by my sixteen-year-old son's hospital bed, anguishing with him in the middle of the night. He'd had full spinal fusion surgery on his back that morning, and bone had been harvested from his hip to aid in repairing the facet joints that had been severed during the procedure. Rather than resting peacefully, Josh was sweating profusely, and his breathing was labored. "Are you praying, Mom?" he whispered. "It hurts so much. Do you think Grandma's praying?"

My heart was breaking for him; I pushed the call button a second time for attention from the intensive care night nurse. Josh had always had a high pain tolerance, and the surgeon had placed an epidural inside the incision, which would allow pain medication to go directly to the wound, eliminating the need for morphine. That all sounded good, but something wasn't right!

The nurse arrived, a bit put out that she had been summoned again. She stated firmly that she had already fed all the allowed medication into the epidural tube and that Josh would just have to wait for more.

Hours went by, and my son's suffering continued. Mopping his brow and quietly praying aloud was the only thing I could do to comfort him. As dawn approached, his pain seemed to intensify. So I switched into patient advocate mode.

"I want a physician called to check on Joshua," I stated firmly. When the nurse tried to convince me it was unnecessary to bother a doctor, I exerted myself a bit more. "I *insist* that a physician be called," I said, feeling like grinding my teeth. "I'm telling you, I know something is not right!"

Within seconds of his arrival, the anesthesiologist discovered that the epidural had somehow been caught on a piece of surgical tape and jerked from the wound. Tragically, all of the pain medication Josh should have received through the tube had soaked uselessly into the heavy bandages around it. Josh was immediately put on a morphine drip, and with great relief I watched my son's strained, exhausted body relax. As I gently wiped his face, I could hear the doctor lecturing the nurse outside the room.

"I should have been called hours ago! No surgery patient at this hospital should ever have to spend a night like that kid has endured!"

That harrowing evening, which seems forever etched in my memory, gives me a sad glimpse at what the mother of Jesus must have experienced watching her firstborn son suffer on the cross of Calvary. She was utterly helpless to change his circumstances.

What were her thoughts, her fears, her frustrations? Where were Jesus' disciples? What would happen to his body?

As desperate and dire as her circumstances were, Mary was blessed to have some precious friends and relatives that stood by her. Let's close this volume of *More Night Whispers* with a look at the women who followed Jesus, especially his own mother and his friend Mary Magdalene, and see how God turned their sorrow into joy.

At and after the Cross

He was dead. It was inconceivable to the man accompanying a small group of women who now huddled together in abject misery. Until Christ's last, halting request for John to take Mary home as part of his own family, John had believed that Jesus would suddenly and dramatically change things around—just like he had changed the lives and circumstances of so many others. But at that last request, John had lost all hope. Now the mournful wail of the mother of his Lord seared his own soul.

The past hour had been terrifying. It had already been dark for some time, but when Jesus died, the ground had rumbled beneath them. Clinging to one another, they had weathered the earthquake—and now the earth was still again. Most of the crowd had fled to their homes; even though the soldiers stood their guard, they trembled with fear. "Surely this man was the Son of God!" one said.

Those grieving at the cross did not know that the temple veil covering the Holy of Holies had been torn in two.

THE STRANGE DARKNESS that had descended over the earth seemed to be dissipating. Mary Magdalene lifted red-rimmed eyes from the misery around her to the hillside in the distance where other women stood together watching and weeping. *They heard his final cry,* she thought. *They too know our precious Lord is dead.*

Mary Magdalene stood near the cross with Jesus' mother, John's mother, whose name was Salome, and another Mary, as well as with John, dear John, who hadn't let them come to this terrifying place alone. Mary Magdalene had been up all night, following the mob, witnessing the treachery of corrupt religious leaders, and seeing her Lord's suffering. Now she turned her gaze to his feet; blood and puss oozed from the wound around the spike. *How many times did I kneel to wash those precious feet,* she thought, longing to kneel once more to wash away the blood, the grime, the pain.

A WAR WAS RAGING within the heart of Mary, the mother of Jesus. Her grief was so sharp she found it difficult to breathe. Grief all the more terrible because she had clung to the belief that in the end, Jesus would turn the terror of the last twenty-four hours into victory.

God! she cried out in her spirit. *Where were you today? How could you, his Father, watch what they did to him and do nothing to stop it? Why didn't Jesus stop it himself? I don't understand! I was honored and obedient to bear your Son, but rather than being blessed among women, I feel cursed! What has happened?*

Her eyes lifted again to her son, her grown-up boy. She wanted to scream at whoever it was who'd made that awful crown. A sob welled up and erupted from within her. His arms that had wrapped around her were now stretched out of the sockets; those precious hands that had patted her face when he was a little boy were now skewered and bloody against a rough post. Her eyes burned with tears, and her heart ached with raw emotion. *And his nakedness for all to see. I can't stand this, God!*

A SMALL CONTINGENT of soldiers arrived, and John, seeing that a heavy mallet was carried by one, shepherded the small group of women farther away from the cross.

"What are they going to do?" Mary Magdalene asked.

"Are they here to remove the bodies?" Salome asked. "The other two on the crosses still seem to be fighting for breath."

"Don't look that way right now!" John said urgently. "We should leave here."

Crack! A soldier swung the mallet against the legs of the thieves hanging helplessly on their crosses. Shrieks of pain rang out. *Crack!*

"What are they doing?" Mary cried, refusing to move away.

John hated to answer. "Since it's almost dusk, they're hurrying up the dying process," he explained quietly. "If the men can't use their legs to lift themselves up, they can't breathe."

Mary held her own breath as the soldiers approached Jesus, but to her relief, they didn't use the mallet on her son.

"This one's already dead," one soldier said. He reached up with his spear and plunged it into Jesus' side. Blood and water poured out from the wound as the small group gasped in horror. Someone vomited. Mary collapsed to her knees, clutching her sides and rocking back and forth as if she had taken the blade herself.

SOMEONE ELSE WAS WATCHING the execution and immediately left the scene to seek an audience with the governor. His name was Joseph of Arimathea, an honest and devout man who had been a secret disciple of Jesus.

"I would like permission to take the body of Jesus Christ and give it a proper burial," Joseph of Arimathea said. "It will soon be evening, and by law, he must be buried."

Pilate looked up in surprise at the man's request. *Isn't this fellow a member of the Jewish council?* he thought to himself. *Perhaps there are some of them with consciences, after all.*

"So he's not to be flung on the dung heap?" Pilate asked crudely. "Is it true, then, that he's dead already?" To be certain, he summoned his centurion, who verified that it was so.

"Very well, you may take the body, although I'd be interested to know why you didn't stand up and make yourself known to me hours ago," he said, shaking his head.

Simply nodding, Joseph left, quickly purchased a roll of linen, and then met with his old friend and colleague, Nicodemus, who had already obtained a large amount of expensive burial spices.

BACK AT THE CROSS, Mary Magdalene had summoned the strength to think beyond the moment. "John, what will happen to the body? By law it must be buried by sunset. How can we get the body? What should we do?"

Just as the group was coming to grips with the dilemma that lay before them, Joseph of Arimathea and an elderly man named Nicodemus arrived with a guard. While Joseph instructed that the spiked feet be released and the crossbar lowered, Nicodemus made his way to John and the women.

"Don't be alarmed," he said kindly, shielding them from the scene. "We are friends, and more important than that, we are believers. We have requested the body of Christ from Pilate, and it would be our great privilege to give our Lord a proper burial. We have come prepared with linen and spices to do that."

"But where will you bury him?" Mary asked anxiously.

"We need to hurry with our task, as the time is short, but be assured that there is a new tomb near here where he will be laid. Go home now, dear woman, and rest, knowing that we will take care of the matter."

John led some of the weary band to his home, but Mary Magdalene and the other Mary, who was the mother of James and Joses, stayed back to see where Jesus would be laid.

With heavy hearts the two men lifted the pierced and lacerated body of their Lord. Dusk was falling, and there was little time to wash or prepare the body, but together they wrapped the corpse, placing large amounts of myrrh and aloes within the linen folds. Then they placed the body in a tomb that was within a garden, not far from where Jesus had been crucified. The tomb was new and belonged to Joseph of Arimathea himself. After finishing their task, they rolled a massive stone over the opening to the tomb, and soldiers, under Pilate's command, guarded the entrance.

Mary Magdalene and the other Mary finally left for the home where the women were staying for Passover week. Although they were frustrated that by law they could not return to the grave until Sunday, their exhausted minds and bodies were desperate for the rest Saturday would allow.

Saturday dragged by for the women. Mary wished she had stayed with Mary Magdalene and the other Mary the night before to see where Joseph and Nicodemus had laid Jesus' body. She and her sister Salome had come back with John and prepared spices that they would use to anoint Jesus' body on Sunday, since it was against the law to do so on the Sabbath. Then, exhausted by the day's horrific events, they had tried to sleep, to little avail.

The others encouraged Mary to rest, but flashbacks haunted her every thought.

She recalled how the sky had been lit by a bright star and shining angels at Jesus' birth, and how, upon his death, the sun had refused to shine. *Why didn't God order angels to slay those who had taken his own Son's life?* she wondered. *And how, after experiencing the miracle of Jesus' birth, will I be able to live with the memory of his death?*

Thinking back to those early days of Jesus' life, she remembered Simeon, the old man who had asked God to allow him to see the Messiah before he died. *Simeon told me this pain was coming,* she thought. *He said that many would speak against Jesus, and that a sword would pierce my own soul too. How little did I realize how painful that sword would be.*

MARY MAGDALENE STARED into the darkness, impatiently waiting for the dawn. It had been so hard to sit through the Sabbath without going to the tomb. She owed Jesus so much that to be denied this last loving act of service to him was devastating.

Her life had been intolerable before she'd met Jesus. But he had freed her from the demonic bondage that had filled her life with fear and loneliness. She had been delivered that day! And what a privilege it had been to join his missionary journey to all the cities and villages around the Sea of Galilee. She had grown rapidly in her faith because Jesus had been a rabbi for women as well as for men. And the fellowship of the other women who had helped support his ministry was precious—they had become like sisters.

She couldn't rest another minute! Getting up quietly, she stepped around the other pallets, careful not to wake Mary, the mother of Jesus, who finally seemed to be in a deep sleep.

Nudging Salome awake, she whispered, "The dawn is almost here! Let's get ready and go to the tomb." She woke the other Mary as well.

With Mary Magdalene leading the way, the women stepped out into the brisk morning air, each carrying a spice box.

"I'm glad to be going early," Salome said. "The earlier we leave these spices with the body, the better. But maybe we should have waited for Peter and John to go with us. I don't think the three of us are strong enough to roll away the stone."

"Don't worry," Mary Magdalene said. "The soldiers will help us. They were posted there on Friday night."

As they approached the Place of the Skull, which still had the vertical poles stuck in the ground, they averted their eyes and didn't speak, skirting around the edge of the area and heading toward the garden and tomb.

"Oh no!" Mary Magdalene cried as the tomb came in view. The stone had been rolled away, and the tomb was wide open. "His body has been stolen! I'll go warn Peter and John!" Dropping her spices in her haste, she ran back to the city and burst into the house.

"I've been to the tomb," she cried breathlessly. "They've taken away the Lord!"

AFTER MARY HAD LEFT, Salome and the other Mary cautiously approached the open tomb. *Where are the guards?* they wondered. The body was obviously gone from the slab where it should have been, but the linens were still there. They glanced at each other with fear in their eyes. Why would someone steal a decaying corpse and leave the scented wrappings behind? It was inconceivable.

Peeking further into the tomb, they were shocked to see an angel, whose appearance was like lightning. He smiled at them and said gently, "Don't be afraid. I know you are looking for Jesus who was crucified. He isn't here; he has risen, just as he said." He gestured to the slab and linens. "Come, see for yourself the place where he lay. Then go quickly and give his disciples this message: 'He has risen from the dead and is going ahead of you into Galilee. There you will see him.'"

The women rushed away, filled with awe and joy.

WHILE THESE THINGS were happening, the guards who had left their post were in the city, reporting to the chief priests what had happened.

"First, there was a quake, and that huge gravestone moved aside of its own accord!" one man babbled. "Then there was this strange man who looked like lightning and sat right on top of the stone. And the body was gone!"

The priests and elders quickly met together and agreed to bribe the guards, offering them a large sum of money to say that Jesus' disciples had come and taken the body away while they were asleep. "If this report gets to the governor, we will satisfy him and keep you out of trouble," they said to the frightened men. So the soldiers took the money and did as they were told.

LEAVING MARY MAGDALENE BEHIND, Peter and John lost no time in racing to the tomb. John was younger than Peter and ran ahead, reaching the tomb first. Stooping down, he looked in and saw the linens, but he didn't step inside. Peter arrived minutes later and entered the tomb without hesitation; John followed. Indeed, the body was gone. The linens were lying there, and they noted that the face cloth that had been bound around Jesus' head was folded neatly and set apart from the other linens. Shaken by these things and not understanding what they meant, the men left for their homes.

CERTAIN THAT THE BODY of her Lord had been stolen, Mary Magdalene made her way back to the tomb, brokenhearted. Grief, frustration, and anger at the callousness of Jesus' enemies welled up inside of her, and as she reached the tomb, she wept aloud.

Where have they taken him? her heart cried. *Wasn't killing him enough?*

Still weeping, she stooped to look inside the tomb and was shocked to see two angels in brilliant white. One was at the head and the other at the feet of where the body of Jesus had been laid. In unison they said to her, "Woman, why are you weeping?"

"Because they have taken away my Lord, and I don't know where they have laid him!"

Turning around, Mary saw a man standing there, and in her grief she didn't even focus on him, assuming he was the gardener.

"Woman, why are you weeping? Whom are you seeking?" he asked.

Wiping her eyes, she sobbed, "Sir, if you have carried his body away, tell me where you have laid him, and I will take him!"

Then he simply and lovingly said her name in the voice she knew so well. "Mary."

She looked up at him, stunned for a moment. It was Jesus! He had risen from the grave!

"Teacher!" she cried, falling at his feet to embrace them.

"Do not cling to me now, Mary," Jesus said gently, "for I have not yet ascended to my Father. Go and tell my brothers."

Nodding in obedience and overflowing with joy, Mary Magdalene ran back to the disciples and reported everything, shouting, "I have seen the Lord!"

Digging Deeper

The followers of Jesus were many, but where were they at his darkest hour? While most of his closest inner circle of disciples disappeared temporarily upon his arrest, others, many of whom were women, were faithful to him to the end of his suffering and were blessed to be the first to see the empty tomb. Other men who had been secret disciples surfaced after his death in a very timely manner.

The disciples would come back to the Savior after his resurrection stronger in their faith than they had ever been, and they would be mightily used by God to establish the early church. But for this last chapter of *More Night Whispers*, I want to focus on those faithful women who never abandoned Jesus. Look with me at his female followers, at the secret disciples who buried him, and at the significance of the torn curtain, and take a glimpse at what followed the resurrection.

Who were the women who followed Jesus? The Bible records that women whose lives had been changed by the ministry of Jesus joined him and his disciples on a missionary journey to all the cities and villages throughout Galilee. Luke 8:1–3 names Mary Magdalene; Joanna, the wife of Cuza, the manager of Herod's household (isn't that a fascinating tidbit of information?); Susanna; "and many others," saying that these women helped support his ministry out of their own means.

From other passages we know that Mary and Martha, who were sisters from Bethany, were also supporters, often opening their home to Christ and his men. It is interesting to note that two mothers, in addition to Mary the mother of Jesus, followed Christ and are listed as women who accompanied their sons on some of these journeys. First there is Mary's sister, Salome, the wife of Zebedee and the mother of both James and John, members of Jesus' inner circle. Second, there is yet another Mary, probably the wife of Clopas, who was the mother of James (another, younger James than the aforementioned) and Joses. (Is your head spinning yet? Mary and James seem to have been very popular names!)

Many of these women had followed Jesus to Jerusalem for the Passover and ultimately to his death on the cross. Their presence and their loyalty to Christ probably offended many Jewish men, most of whom would never touch or even speak to a woman—including their own wife—in public. Jesus had dared to do both (John 4:27 and Luke 13:11–13).

Those who stood with Mary, Jesus' mother, at the cross are her sister Salome, Mary the wife of Clopas, Mary Magdalene, and John (John 19:25). After Jesus' burial at dusk on Friday, the women were prohibited from going to the grave and anointing the body until Sunday, the first day of the week, because such activity was prohibited on Saturday, the Sabbath. Lawrence O. Richards explains this law, according to the Mishnah, which is a six-part code of rules intended to govern the daily life and worship of the Jews: "A woman should not go out with . . . a spice box, or . . . with a perfume flask, and if she went out, she is liable to a sin offering."[1]

The women listed by Mark as having gone to the grave on Sunday morning to anoint the body of Christ with spices are Mary Magdalene, Mary the mother of James, and Salome (Mark 16:1). These women had loved Christ, served him in his ministry, suffered with him as they witnessed his crucifixion, grieved together at his death, and rejoiced together with his resurrection. You've met Mary the mother of Jesus in earlier chapters. Let's acquaint ourselves with Mary Magdalene, who is mentioned more times in the Bible than any other woman with regard to Jesus' earthly ministry.

Who was Mary Magdalene? After Jesus freed her from the torment of seven demons, Mary Magdalene became one of Jesus' most faithful and grateful followers. She was often referred to as "The Magdalene," which indicates she was from the area of Magdala, a prosperous city located on the shoreline of the Sea of Galilee, about three miles from Capernaum. Over the centuries, people have mistakenly accepted that Mary Magdalene was also a reformed prostitute, but every commentary I studied on the subject insisted that such an allegation is baseless, stating that Scripture does not back up that notion. The scholar Herbert Lockyer comments, "The wide acceptance of the tradition that she was a reformed prostitute is utterly baseless."[2]

Mary Magdalene was not only a grateful woman, but she was also a woman of financial means. We are not told her age or if she was a widow, but she was free to follow Jesus with the others who supported his ministry financially. A note in the New International Version Student Bible explains that "in the Middle East of that day, teachers traveled from town to town, accepting the gifts of appreciative listeners. Luke points out that certain women who had been healed by Jesus helped provide for him. In all, Luke introduces 13 women who do not appear in the other Gospels."[3]

Mary was also a leader. Lockyer notes that

she is mentioned fourteen times in the gospels. . . . A striking feature in eight of the fourteen passages is that Mary is named in connection with other women, but she always heads the list, implying that she occupied the place at the front of service rendered by godly females. In the five times where she is mentioned alone, the connection is with the death and resurrection of Christ

(Mark 16:9; John 20:1, 11, 16, 18). In one instance her name comes after that of the mother of Jesus.[4]

Scripture records that she followed the trial of Christ and was present at the cross with John, Jesus' mother, Jesus' aunt, and another Mary. Her greatest joy—even greater than being freed from demonic bondage—was meeting Christ in the garden after his resurrection. She was the very first person to see and to speak with him. Her final words in Scripture are breathlessly triumphant: "I have seen the Lord!" (John 20:18).

Who were the good guys who unexpectedly showed up at the end of the day on Friday? They were Joseph of Arimathea and Nicodemus, both secret believers before the amazing events surrounding the death of Christ, and bold, active believers afterward. These two men had the privilege of taking the body of their Lord from the cross and preparing it for burial in Joseph of Arimathea's own tomb. Preparing bodies was usually women's work, and it was most certainly defiling work. For them in particular, it was politically risky work.

But after Jesus died, those things no longer mattered. Joseph and Nicodemus probably didn't even realize until later that they were part of the fulfillment of a prophecy from the Old Testament regarding Jesus. It had been foretold in Isaiah 53:9 that the Messiah would receive a rich man's burial. Most ordinary people were buried in the ground; only the wealthy had tombs. But these men, under very rushed circumstances (because the Sabbath was rapidly approaching), wrapped the body of Jesus in one hundred pounds of expensive spices and laid him in a brand-new tomb (John 19:39–40 KJV).

Nicodemus was an elderly, rather wealthy religious leader who was part of the Jewish council, and he was a Pharisee who sought Jesus out at night to ask him questions about how he could be born again. In John 3 we see Nicodemus as a cautious enquirer with a heart that hungers for truth, and in John 7:45–52 as a lonely voice that speaks up in defense of Jesus before the high priests and Pharisees and gets mocked for his comment. Then we read in John 19:39–40 that Nicodemus openly joined Joseph of Arimathea in preparing Christ's body for burial.

Joseph of Arimathea was a rich and respected member of the Sanhedrin, the Jewish supreme court. He was an honestly devout man, and he lived a life of integrity. He also was one of those who never forgot the promises prophesied by the Old Testament prophets, and he lived in anticipation of the reign of the promised Messiah. Mark wrote that he was an honorable counselor (Mark 15:43 KJV), Luke reported that he was both "good" and "just" (Luke 23:50–51 KJV), and John tells us that like Nicodemus, he was a secret disciple of Jesus (John 19:38). Herbert Lockyer in his *All the Men of the Bible* says

> Joseph of Arimathaea was similar to Nicodemus in his respect for our Lord as a man, admiration for Him as a teacher, belief in Him as the Christ, and yet. . . . Dreading the hostility of his colleagues on the Sanhedrin, he kept his faith secret.[5]

That is, until Jesus died. Conscience and conviction kicked in, as well as a boldness he had lacked before. Risking the criticism of the Sanhedrin, Joseph personally sought an audience with Pilate himself and earnestly requested that he be allowed to inter the body of Christ before the sun set. Then he and Nicodemus joined forces to reverently pay their last respects to the Savior.

What was the significance of the torn curtain? Many unusual events surrounded the death of Christ. The sky became black for six hours, an earthquake shook the earth when he died, and the veil enclosing the most holy place in the temple ripped in half (Matt. 27:51). Jesus died at approximately 3:00 in the afternoon, which was the time when the high priest (Caiaphas) was about to enter the Holy of Holies. This place in the temple was for God alone and was separated from the rest of the temple by a very large, thick curtain. Herbert Lockyer in his article "The Miracles at Calvary" describes this curtain and its significance:

> This veil was reckoned to be a hand-breadth in thickness and woven of seventy-two twisted plaits, each plait consisting of twenty-four threads. It was sixty feet long and thirty wide. Two of them were made every year, and 400 priests were needed to manipulate a veil.
>
> The significant feature here is that the veil was rent "from the top," not from the bottom, meaning, of course that it was rent by God, not man.
>
> The barrier between God and man was destroyed. The Temple and the old ceremonial form of worship were no longer needed. A new and living way was opened into the presence of God. From that moment, the cross became that which admitted to, or excluded from, the Holy Place, according to the relation men [and women] bore to Christ (Heb. 9:8; 10:19–31).[6]

I try to imagine Caiaphas, decked out in ceremonial robe and headpiece, approaching the holy place to perform a ritual that had been performed by every high priest before him—and having the liver scared right out of him when the earth shook and the curtain tore before his eyes! Sadly, Scripture gives no evidence that he changed his evil ways.

The good news is that God no longer requires blood sacrifices, because his Son paid the price once and for all. The only requirement is accepting Jesus Christ and the payment he made on the cross, by faith, and inviting the risen Lord to be your own Savior.

What happened after the resurrection? The New Testament writers recorded ten occasions when Jesus appeared to his followers. One of those occasions is known as the Great Commission, in which Jesus commissioned the eleven remaining disciples (who were now known as apostles) to go into all the world and make disciples, baptizing, healing, and teaching in his name. You can read about it in Matthew 28. At his last appearance to his apostles, he ascended into heaven (Luke 24:49–53), promising that he would return one day and that the Holy Spirit would come to them. This promise was fulfilled, and the exciting story of the empowered new Christian Church (which included both men and women who were filled with the Holy Spirit) is found in Acts 1 and 2.

How can this story apply to your life?

God rewards those who are faithful. Women during the time of Christ had few societal rights and even fewer religious rights. The Life Application Bible notes:

> These women could do very little. They couldn't speak before the Sanhedrin in Jesus' defense; they couldn't appeal to Pilate; they couldn't stand against the crowds; they couldn't overpower the Roman guards. But they did what they could. They stayed at the cross when the disciples had fled; they followed Jesus' body to the tomb; and they prepared spices for his body. Because these women used the opportunities they had, they were the first to witness the resurrection. God blessed their devotion.[7]

You may feel that what you have to offer to God isn't much compared to the talent, resources, or influence of others, but remember that God honors faithfulness and he sees the attitude of our hearts.

Don't let leadership go to your head. Caiaphas is a prime example of someone who was given a position of great honor and then defiled the sacredness of the position. Today we sometimes hear of church leaders who misuse their positions of influence. As God allows you to move into positions of authority or influence, don't abuse the opportunity! Choose to represent Christ rather than yourself.

Trust in God's promises and keep the faith. Even those closest to Jesus misunderstood God's plan in sending the Messiah. Jesus had told his disciples that he would die and rise again, but in the pain of the moment, they forgot those promises and lost hope. Don't make the same mistake when you face difficult circumstances that you don't understand. Take God at his Word, and keep trusting in his promises, remembering that Jesus never fails.

As I think back over this story, I am struck by the devotion of the women whose lives Jesus had miraculously changed. And after speaking at a recent conference, I was reminded that God is still in the business of changing lives. A lovely young woman handed me an envelope as she was leaving. I read the letter on my flight home and found myself soberly marveling at the power God has to change and heal wounded souls. With her permission, I share her letter here, so that if you're in need of the touch of the Savior like she was, or like Mary Magdalene or the other women who followed Jesus, you'll reach out to the risen Savior tonight.

My name is Rita, and I grew up on a small dairy farm with 9 brothers and 2 sisters. I was the 11th of 12 children. My earliest childhood memories are of watching my dad push my mom into a corner and raise his hand to her, being pinned down on the floor myself and whipped with a 3-inch leather belt, or being passed around naked from one brother to the next as each took turns satisfying their sexual curiosity in the barn. I lived the majority of my childhood living in fear—always planning my next move to make sure I would be safe.

A typical day in my childhood started the minute my brothers were all in the barn milking cows. My heart would race with fear as I jumped out of bed at 5:00 a.m. I'd unlock my bedroom door, peer out to make sure one of my brothers hadn't pretended to be sick that morning in order to catch me, and then I'd run downstairs and sit by my elderly, alcoholic grandpa, who was my only source of safety until the school bus came.

Abuse by my family members gave me a very warped image of God. We were a churchgoing family, so I knew about God. On particularly bad nights I would pound my pillow and plead with him to please "let me die!" When he didn't answer my prayer, I assumed he didn't love me and that I must have done something to deserve this life.

During high school I got involved in as many activities as I could, avoiding home completely. I was finally getting the approval I desperately longed for and seemed to have it all together, but on the inside, I was my own worst enemy and critic. The stage was being set for my long search to find any kind of love and acceptance—healthy or not.

In college my world came crashing down around me. I was so used to living two separate lives—happy and energetic on the outside but lonely, fearful, and angry at home. Dorm life started to feel suffocating, and during my sophomore year I suddenly stopped eating. I knew I needed help, and went to talk to the hall director and ended up spilling my entire story.

Two significant things happened that night. He insisted that I begin intensive counseling to help me deal with my past, but he also introduced me to a side of God I had never met before. He told me about Jesus Christ. He said that Jesus loved me so much he died for me. I believed what he said. From then on I sensed that God was "pursuing" me to turn my life over to him, but I wasn't ready yet to completely trust him.

For six years I continued with a double life, going to church, partying, and eventually pouring myself into a busy career, occasionally seeking God between boyfriends. Then, when the man of my dreams called off our wedding, I reached my turning point and gave in to God. "I give up, Lord," I said. "You have control of my life." It was then that I saw God's unconditional love for me for the first time and knew that my life with him was just beginning. My double life had finally ended!

God began to teach me things I thought were impossible, like forgiveness for those who had hurt me. He showed me that forgiveness is a command, not a feeling. When I obeyed and forgave others, his love melted away the anger and hate I had for my family. This was key to my healing process. I also learned that the chain of abuse passed down in my family is not a human chain but rather a chain of slavery put on by the king of evil—Satan—and that Christ is the only one who can break those chains.

I also learned that the past does not determine my future— God does! I know without doubt that he is in control, he loves me, and he has a plan and purpose for everything in my life. And, finally, Jeremiah 29:13 says, "You will seek me and find me when you seek me with all your heart." This verse taught me that when I put God first in my life—even before my own healing—his overwhelming love fills me so completely that I am able to rise above the painful memories of the past and live a life full of love and peace. Before Christ I had nothing. Now I have everything!

A Whispered Prayer

Dear Heavenly Father, thank you for being victorious over death itself! Thank you for the example of faithful women whose broken lives you healed, rescued, saved—who, once freed from their pasts, served you without reservation. I want to be that kind of committed woman of God. I want to be bold in my faith and not a "secret" disciple. Please help me to live for you every day. In the precious name of Jesus, Amen.

Get Up and Go Ideas for Tomorrow

1. I will go to a Christian bookstore or go online to order a book on Bible promises. Beginning tomorrow, I will take the time to read a page each day and stop to thank God for his faithfulness to all those who believe.
2. The next time discouragement creeps into my life, I will recall this story, give the situation to God, and remember that he can turn my sadness into joy.

A Thought to Ponder as I Fall Asleep

Like Mary Magdalene weeping in the garden, do I get so consumed with my problems that I don't even recognize that God is standing right beside me?

The Scripture Reading: John 19:31–42; Luke 24:1–12; John 20:10–18

Now it was the day of Preparation, and the next day was to be a special Sabbath. Because the Jews did not want the bodies left on the crosses during the Sabbath, they asked Pilate to have the legs broken and the bodies taken down. The soldiers therefore came and broke the legs of the first man who had been crucified with Jesus, and then those of the other. But when they came to Jesus and found that he was already dead, they did not break his legs. Instead, one of the soldiers pierced Jesus' side with a spear, bringing a sudden flow of blood and water. The man who saw it has given testimony, and his testimony is true. He knows that he tells the truth, and he testifies so that you also may believe. These things happened so that the Scripture would be fulfilled: "Not one of his bones will be broken," and, as another Scripture says, "They will look on the one they have pierced."

Later, Joseph of Arimathea asked Pilate for the body of Jesus. Now Joseph was a disciple of Jesus, but secretly because he feared the Jews. With Pilate's permission, he came and took the body away. He was accompanied by Nicodemus, the man who earlier had visited Jesus at night. Nicodemus brought a mixture of myrrh and aloes, about seventy-five pounds. Taking Jesus' body, the two of them wrapped it, with the spices, in strips of linen. This was in accordance with Jewish burial customs. At the place where Jesus was crucified, there was a garden, and in the garden a new tomb, in which no one had ever been laid. Because it was the Jewish day of Preparation and since the tomb was nearby, they laid Jesus there....

On the first day of the week, very early in the morning, the women took the spices they had prepared and went to the tomb. They found the stone rolled away from the tomb, but when they entered, they did not find the body of the Lord Jesus. While they were wondering about this, suddenly two men in clothes that gleamed like lightning stood beside them. In their fright the women bowed down with their faces to the ground, but the men said to them, "Why do you look for the living among the dead? He is not here; he has risen! Remember how he told you, while he was still with you in Galilee: 'The Son of Man must be delivered into the hands of sinful men, be crucified and on the third day be raised again.' " Then they remembered his words.

When they came back from the tomb, they told all these things to the Eleven and to all the others. It was Mary Magdalene, Joanna, Mary the mother of James, and the others with them who told this to the apostles. But they did not believe the women, because their words seemed to them like nonsense. Peter, however, got up and ran to the tomb. Bending over, he saw the strips of linen lying by themselves, and he went away, wondering to himself what had happened....

Then the disciples went back to their homes, but Mary stood outside the tomb crying. As she wept, she bent over to look into the tomb and saw two angels in white, seated where Jesus' body had been, one at the head and the other at the foot.

They asked her, "Woman, why are you crying?"

"They have taken my Lord away," she said, "and I don't know where they have put him."

At this, she turned around and saw Jesus standing there, but she did not realize that it was Jesus.

"Woman," he said, "why are you crying? Who is it you are looking for?"

Thinking he was the gardener, she said, "Sir, if you have carried him away, tell me where you have put him, and I will get him."

Jesus said to her, "Mary."

She turned toward him and cried out in Aramaic, "Rabboni!" (which means Teacher).

Jesus said, "Do not hold on to me, for I have not yet returned to the Father. Go instead to my brothers and tell them, 'I am returning to my Father and your Father, to my God and your God.'"

Mary Magdalene went to the disciples with the news: "I have seen the Lord!" And she told them that he had said these things to her.

Final Note: Although portions from both John and Luke's account of the burial and resurrection of Jesus Christ are given above, refer to the accounts given by all four Gospel writers, Matthew, Mark, Luke, and John, for the entire story.

Notes

Chapter 1: The Awakening

1. "Where Was the Garden of Eden?" The Word in Life Study Bible (Nashville: Thomas Nelson, 1996), 9.

2. "God Limits Evil," The Word in Life Study Bible, 15.

3. Max Lucado, A Love Worth Giving (Nashville: W Publishing Group, 2002), 120.

4. Walter A. Elwell, Baker Commentary on the Bible (Grand Rapids: Baker, 1989), 14.

5. Michael Kendrick and Daryl Lucas, eds., 365 Life Lessons from Bible People (Wheaton: Tyndale, 1996), 2.

6. Lucado, 121.

7. "Vital Statistics," Life Application Bible, New International Version (Wheaton: Tyndale and Grand Rapids: Zondervan, 1991), page unnumbered.

Chapter 2: Multicolored Jealousy

1. Life Application Bible, 78.

2. Life Application Bible (30-day journey figure taken from a study note for 37:28), 78.

3. Ralph Gower, The New Manners and Customs of Bible Times (Chicago: Moody Press, 1987), 57.

4. Life Application Bible, 76.

5. Gower, 58.

6. Herbert Lockyer, Sr., Nelson's Illustrated Bible Dictionary (Nashville: Thomas Nelson, 1986), 237.

7. Gower, 201.

8. "Consider This," The Word in Life Study Bible, 107.

9. Life Application Bible study note on Joseph, 77.

10. Bruce Wilkinson and Kenneth Boa, Talk Thru the Old Testament (Nashville: Thomas Nelson, 1983), 5.

Chapter 3: Good Guy, Bad Times

1. Edith Deen, *All the Women of the Bible* (San Francisco: Harper & Row, 1955), 45–46.
2. Elwell, 32.
3. Ibid.
4. Life Application Bible, 82.

Chapter 4: The Risky Reunion

1. Elwell, 33.
2. A. R. Fausset, *Fausset's Bible Dictionary* (Grand Rapids: Zondervan, 1981), 394.
3. Rabbi Joseph Telushkin, *Biblical Literacy* (New York: William Morrow and Company, 1997), 83.
4. *The New Scofield Reference Bible* (New York: Oxford University Press, 1967), 1.

Chapter 5: Lost and Found

1. The Word in Life Study Bible, 786.
2. Herbert Lockyer, *All the Men of the Bible* (Grand Rapids: Zondervan, 1958), 207.
3. Matthew Henry, *Matthew Henry's Commentary on the Whole Bible* (London: Fisher edition, 1845), 1: 994.
4. Lockyer, 71.
5. William MacDonald, *Believer's Bible Commentary* (Nashville: Thomas Nelson, 1990), 418.
6. Deen, 144.
7. Ibid., 145.
8. "For Your Info," The Word in Life Study Bible, 680.
9. Telushkin, 273.
10. Kendrick and Lucas, 191.
11. Elwell, 260.

Chapter 6: Mixed Blessings

1. Gower, 65.
2. Deen, 160.
3. Ibid., 162.
4. Gower, 63.
5. Ibid., 65.
6. Deen, 162.
7. Lockyer, *Nelson's Illustrated Bible Dictionary*, 1009.
8. MacDonald, 1368.

Chapter 7: The Runaway Bride (and Groom and Baby)

1. Deen, 172.
2. Gower, 62–63.
3. Ibid., 63.
4. Elwell, 726.
5. Ibid.
6. Lockyer, *All the Men of the Bible*, 144.
7. Howard F. Vos, *Nelson's New Illustrated Bible Manners and Customs* (Nashville: Thomas Nelson, 1999), 392.
8. The Word in Life Study Bible, 1614.

Chapter 8: The Untouchables

1. "Untouchables," *National Geographic*, June 2003, 2.
2. Ibid., 9.
3. Lockyer, *Nelson's Illustrated Bible Dictionary*, 402.
4. *The New Testament and Wycliffe Bible Commentary*, produced for Moody Monthly (New York: The Iversen Associates, 1971), 133.
5. "A Respected Leader Takes a Risk," The Word in Life Study Bible, 1726.
6. Ibid., 1646.
7. MacDonald, 1333.
8. Matthew Henry, *Matthew Henry's Commentary on the Whole Bible* (Marshallton, DE: The National Foundation for Christian Education, 1845), 3: 72.
9. The Word in Life Study Bible, 1645.

Chapter 9: Countdown to Mission Accomplished

1. J. I. Packer, Merrill C. Tenney, and William White, Jr., *Nelson's Illustrated Encyclopedia of Bible Facts* (Nashville: Thomas Nelson, 1995), 524.
2. Ibid., 526.
3. Ibid.
4. Life Application Bible, 1853.
5. Fausset, 105.
6. Ibid.
7. Ibid., 573.
8. Ibid., 573–74.
9. Life Application Bible, 1775.
10. Vos, 441–43.
11. Fausset, 145.
12. Carol Kent, *Speak Up with Confidence* (Colorado Springs: NavPress, 1997), 177–78.

Chapter 10: Aftershock and Awesome Joy

1. Lawrence O. Richards, *The Victor Bible Background Commentary, New Testament* (Colorado Springs: Victor Chariot Publishing, 1985), 54.

2. Herbert Lockyer, *All the Women of the Bible* (Grand Rapids: Zondervan, n.d.), 100.

3. The Student Bible, New International Version (Grand Rapids: Zondervan, 1986), 905.

4. Lockyer, *All the Women of the Bible*, 100.

5. Lockyer, *All the Men of the Bible*, 204.

6. Herbert Lockyer, *All the Miracles of the Bible* (Grand Rapids: Zondervan, 1961), 244.

7. Life Application Bible, 1778.

As a motivational speaker, trainer, and storyteller, **Jennie Afman Dimkoff** speaks throughout the United States and Canada for conferences and retreats. She is the president of Storyline Ministries, Inc., and is the author and storyteller for Kids' Time, a children's audiocassette ministry. Jennie also serves on the staff of Speak Up With Confidence seminars.

Married to her best friend, probate court judge Graydon W. Dimkoff, Jennie is "Mom" to their two grown children, Amber and Josh. She believes that the Christian woman should choose to be God's woman in every phase of life and is committed to serving as a Christian leader in her community and beyond. She currently serves as a board committee member for Gerber Memorial Health Services, is a member of the board of trustees for Cornerstone University, and serves as a board member for AWSA, the Advanced Writer's and Speaker's Association.

Jennie is a member of the National Speakers' Association and has been a keynote speaker at arena events, including Heritage Keepers and Time Out for Women. In conference and retreat settings, whether large or small, her in-depth teaching is generously seasoned with her gifted storytelling, leaving audiences greatly entertained, deeply moved, and highly motivated.

Jennie is represented by Speak Up Speaker Services. For information on scheduling her to speak for your organization, go to her website at www.storylineministries.com, or contact:

Speak Up Speaker Services
Call toll-free (888) 870-7719
Email: speakupinc@aol.com